MEDIEVAL AND RENAISSANCE SPIRITUALITY

DISCOVERING THE TREASURES OF THE GREAT MASTERS

MARIA JAOUDI

Paulist Press
New York/Mahwah, NJ

The Scripture quotations contained herein are from the New Revised Standard Version: Catholic Edition Copyright © 1989 and 1993, by the Division of Christian Education of the National Council of the Churches of Christ in the United States of America. Used by permission. All rights reserved.

Cover and book design by Lynn Else

Library of Congress Cataloging-in-Publication Data

Jaoudi, Maria.
    Medieval and Renaissance spirituality : discovering the treasures of the great masters / Maria Jaoudi.
        p. cm.
    Includes bibliographical references.
    ISBN 978-0-8091-4659-8 (alk. paper)
    1. Religions. 2. Spirituality. I. Title.
    BL80.3.J36 2010
    204'.22—dc22

                                                            2009052224

Published by Paulist Press
997 Macarthur Boulevard
Mahwah, New Jersey 07430

www.paulistpress.com

Printed and bound in the
United States of America

CONTENTS

For Harrison,
"L'amor che move il sole e l'altre stelle."
—*Paradiso*, Canto XXXIII:145
("The love that moves the sun and other stars.")

ART CREDITS

Cover: Rose Window, Abbey of St-Denis, Paris. Photo Bart Parren/iStockphoto.

Chapter 1: Matthias Grünewald, *Resurrection of Christ*. Photo Scala / Art Resource, NY.

Chapter 2: Gian Lorenzo Bernini, *The Ecstasy of Saint Teresa* (close-up). Photo Scala / Art Resource, NY.

Chapter 3: *Sefirot*. From *Zohar: The Book of Enlightenment*, translated and introduced by Daniel Chanan Matt, Classics of Western Spirituality (Mahwah/New York: Paulist Press, 1983).

Chapter 4: Interior of Chartres Cathedral. Photo JurgaR/iStockphoto.

Chapter 5: Giotto, *Dante* (detail from the *Last Judgment*). Photo Scala / Art Resource, NY.

Chapter 6: *The Trinity* (after Hildegard of Bingen). From *Hildegard of Bingen: Scivias*, translated by Mother Columba Hart and Jane Bishop, Classics of Western Spirituality (Mahwah/New York: Paulist Press, 1990).

Chapter 7: *Arabian Circle Pattern*. Image Roland Warmbier/iStockphoto.

Chapter 8: Raphael, *Madonna of the Goldfinch*. Photo Scala / Art Resource. Michelangelo, *David* (detail). Photo Tina Lorien/iStockphoto.

Chapter 9: Jacopo Robusti Tintoretto, *Presentation of Mary in the Temple* (detail). Photo Cameraphoto Arte, Venice/Art Resource, NY.

ACKNOWLEDGEMENTS

Deepest gratitude to Reverend Lawrence Boadt, CSP, Dr. Nancy de Flon, Harry Smith, and Harrison Smith-Jaoudi for help with the manuscript.

Also, thanks are due to my colleagues: Professor Rosalie Amer of Salam Mosque and Cosumnes River College, and Dr. Robert Platzner of Congregation B'nai Israel and the Department of Humanities and Religious Studies, California State University Sacramento, for our continuing work together in the field of Interreligious Dialogue.

Alice, Barbara, Ed, Michael, Stephen, Anna Jaoudi; Hélène, Najla, Ann, Peter Tanous; Helen and Kamal Samhan; thank you for being such a caring family.

INTRODUCTION

Most human beings want to know the purpose for their existence. We want to know why we are in this vast universe and what we can create in our lifetime with our talents and relationships. If we seek oneness with the Divine, we endeavor to live a peaceful and prayerful life. We seek the presence of God in the small and the large, we learn about the nature of God revealed in people and the natural world around us, and we seek to construct a life that is fulfilling.

Throughout the world, human beings have tried to make sense of life on earth and the mysteries connected to life and death. When we connect with the Sacred, we experience significance and allow ourselves to surrender to, and express, the mystery of the spiritual. We are not afraid of surrender; rather, we regard surrender to the spiritual as an avenue of freedom and disclosure of the eternal presence, our true home.

This book concentrates on the Middle Ages and the Renaissance, studying how people of the time created meaning in their life and expressed that meaning through religion and the humanities. The symbolic and allegorical thought-world of the Middle Ages, characterized by a strong belief in the immanence of the supernatural, gradually gave way to the humanism of the Renaissance, with its emphasis on naturalism. The theology and spirituality of these time periods, evidence of a people's striving to understand the Transcendent, have been communicated to us in writings but also through the visual and plastic arts.

This book seeks to display the theology and spirituality of the Middle Ages and the Renaissance in the three major Western religious traditions: Judaism, Christianity, and Islam. Through the architecture of Europe's cathedrals, the work of the remarkable medieval women Julian and Hildegard, the *sefirot* of the Jewish *Kabbalah*, the poetry of Islamic love mystics Rabi'a and Rumi, the paintings of the Florentine masters of the Renaissance, and the art of many others, we share in the attempts to fathom and celebrate the Unfathomable: humanity's never-ending search for God.

Chapter 1

SEEKING GOD: CHRISTIAN CULTURE

In medieval Europe, existential meaning had to do with forging the connection to the spiritual realm. People walked their way to the spiritual, embarking on pilgrimages; they built their way to the spiritual realm, creating the magnificence of gothic cathedrals; and people prayed their way to the spiritual realm through their intense faith.

In this chapter we will examine the flowering of faith in several medieval traditions. We will discover that medieval theology is like a sublime stained-glass window that illumines, and is illumined by, such towering monuments to the spiritual as the architecture of the cathedrals, works by artists such as Giotto painting Francis of Assisi's Christ-likeness, and the revelations of innovative mystics like Julian of Norwich.

Pilgrimage

Pilgrimage was an important religious practice in the Middle Ages. Life was unbearably horrific for most. Women commonly died in their early twenties, men by thirty. Imagine a world with little cleanliness and many cruelties, from torturing kittens to disregarding children's basic needs, which scholars attribute to the fact that parents were detached from their feelings because most children died at an early age. People were truly desperate for an ideal haven-heaven.

In the Christian tradition, pilgrimage was one way to escape physically from the unending injustices and tragedies of daily life. For example, women, who were barred from most occupations and were not taught to read and write, were nevertheless allowed to journey on pilgrimage. Pilgrimage was the only way to extricate oneself from the numbing dreadfulness of life.

Pilgrims usually journeyed to shrines containing the relics of saints in order to ask favors of the saint, often for recovery from illness. Proximity to the saint's relics was thought to gain the pilgrim a special hearing with her or his patron. Some pilgrimages, however, fulfilled a desire to visit Rome or the Holy Land.

One of the most important pilgrimage sites was Santiago de Compostela in Spain, where the tomb of Saint James the Greater (son of Zebedee) is supposedly located. The Romanesque cathedral there was built between 1078 and 1211 CE. People today may still walk the *camino*; some travel with the bare necessities, walking the same route as pilgrims did almost one thousand years ago, testifying to an indescribable holy presence that unites them with the very earth they are traversing. Exemplary pilgrims choose simplicity by not carrying more than a backpack, which adds to the experience of being one with fellow Christians from past centuries.

The pilgrimage routes that crisscrossed Europe were lined with abbeys, priories, monasteries, and hospices. Many were built approximately twenty miles apart because this was the average pilgrim's daily progress. People slept in big open halls that also contained chapels for religious services. And religious charity was made available for the poor, the sick, and for the burial of corpses.

Major churches—"pilgrimage churches"—were pilgrimage destinations. There were five great Romanesque pilgrimage churches:

Saint Martin in Tours, and Saint-Martial in Limoges, both no longer in existence. Saint-Sernin in Toulouse, Saint-Foy in Conques, and Santiago de Compostela may still be visited today.

Romanesque architecture is called "Romanesque" because it relies on the Roman elements of the basilica plan: for example, rounded arches, vaulted ceilings, thick columns to support the weight of the ceilings and walls, and sturdy walls. Saint-Sernin in Toulouse has a typical Romanesque nave. The nave is in the shape of the Latin cross, with chapels that radiate out from the top of the cross. The vaulting is made of stone, which gives Romanesque churches an advantage over early Christian basilicas that were made of wood and thus frequently destroyed by fire. Ideal for music, the stone vault created reverberating effects, which made for superb acoustics and certainly enhanced the effectiveness of Gregorian and other forms of chant.

Characteristics of Gothic Architecture

Gothic architecture, which originated with the pilgrimage church at Vézelay about 1100, embodies mathematical proportions in a search for ever-increasing luminosity. Exterior or flying buttresses supported translucent walls of stained glass. The stories told through the medium of stained glass served as a visual form of education for 90 percent of the population, who could neither read nor write. How they were able to see much of the stained glass is a conundrum, for one needs powerful binoculars to distinguish the details in the stained glass above approximately ten feet.

Most of the stories and personalities portrayed in stained glass were biblical. Heaven and hell were just as real to the medieval mind as the realities of daily life. The description of the Last Judgment, for example, was taken literally and, hence, was effective well into Renaissance times as a theme to help the wayward turn back to God. Michelangelo's last frescoes in the Sistine Chapel portray a muscular Christ, more humane, to be sure, than earlier medieval portrayals, yet just as morally demanding.[1]

The idea of turning back to a forgiving God resonated strongly with medieval people. Hence one of the most popular stories depicted in stained glass by the medieval artisans was the parable of the prodigal son from Luke 15. The prodigal son was sometimes portrayed as a nobleman, wearing a purple gown, riding a gray horse, and with a falcon on his hand. At Bourges Cathedral, for example, people were appalled that a person from the upper class would become a swineherd. Shades of purple, yellow, and green, mixed with blue, red, and white, depict the universal child archetype—albeit more poignantly in medieval times—who must safely return home to the awaiting beneficent and generous arms of the Parent-God.

God Is Light

Who was this Parent-God to a medieval human being? For some, undoubtedly, a parent who forgives their child's waywardness. For others, a forgiving parent, but also a transcendent God symbolized by a new architecture of disappearing walls and the sublime presence of jeweled light. During World War II, this light may have moved the community of Chartres to remove by hand every piece of stained glass and store it in barns until the danger of bombing was over. People were motivated to rise to noble deeds for the sake of preserving great beauty.

Near Paris, at Saint Denis around 1137, the Benedictine Abbot Suger developed an entire theology that supports the Gothic style of architecture. Saint Denis became the royal abbey where French kings are buried and from which Suger's theology gave birth to a prototype for Gothic architecture. For Suger—

who believed that the invisible Spirit is made visible in stone, light, and tinted glass—the light that streams through the windows of a Gothic cathedral, the light we call jeweled, radiant, soft, intense, carries us gloriously from the mundane cares of the world to the profound conscious awareness of God's presence. For Abbot Suger this light really was different spatially and temporally. Perhaps he was right.

French historian George Duby observes that Suger gave birth to "an art of light, clarity, and dazzling radiance."[2] Hoping to create an entrance to the heavenly Jerusalem, Suger realized this lofty concept through the architectural medium we call Gothic, which was characterized by verticality and light. The Gothic style was originally called the "French style"; Giorgio Vasari, in the early sixteenth century, was one of the first to apply the term *Gothic* to it, reflecting the later view that this style was rude and barbaric.

If architecture is a mirror of religious belief, then surely what we have in Gothic architecture is Christ as light. In Abbot Suger's own words:

> Whoever you may be, if you wish to pay homage to these doors, admire not their gold nor their cost, but instead the work they represent and the art. Like gold, a noble achievement gleams, but it gleams nobly; may it enlighten men's minds and may its true lights lead them to the true light of which Christ is the true gateway.[3]

Incarnation

The incarnational dimension Suger so emphasized in the visible matter of the cathedral found a match in the slowly evolving depiction of the suffering Jesus in paintings. The humanity of Christ was identifiable through the body tormented on the cross. We will examine shortly Giotto's fourteenth-century artistic renditions, which, for the first time in many centuries, depicted the range of human emotions. First let us explore an artistic example of extreme human identification with the suffering of Jesus—the sixteenth-century artist Matthias Grünewald's *Isenheim Altarpiece* (fig. 1).

Grünewald[4] was commissioned by the Antonite order in Isenheim to paint a scene with which the patients at their hospital could identify, both psychologically and spiritually. Numerous patients suffered from a dreadful disease called "Saint Anthony's Fire" that was caused by a poisonous fungus in rye flour and often reached epidemic proportions. At that time, people did not understand the disease's origin; those who contracted it suffered terribly from gangrenous skin boils and spasms, eventually resulting in death.

Thomas Mann described Grünewald's wrenching crucifix scene as "among the strongest that ever came before my eyes."[5] J. K. Huysmans declared that "it was 'as if a typhoon of art had been let loose', and was sweeping you away....The Isenheim patients could have no doubt about his suffering."[6] The patients knew that "Another had suffered more."[7]

Jesus' hands are gnarled and wrenching in agony, his taut facial muscles unable to relax into the stillness of death. The pain pulls at every muscle. Jesus' skin is portrayed with innumerable skin lesions, something with no basis in biblical literature, but it certainly must have helped the Isenheim patients who gazed at the suffering Christ as they themselves progressed through to their own terrifying end.

For the Christian Grünewald, this was not the end. The lamb in the forefront at the foot of the cross, resting its foot on a chalice with a cross, depicts the sacrifice necessary to enter the

Fig. 1: Matthias Grünewald
(1455–1528), *Resurrection of Christ.*

next spiritual stage toward resurrection. When the panels of the altarpiece swing open, what we see theologically is a realistic Christian version of redemptive suffering and death leading to new life in the resurrection. The depiction of Christ in Grünewald's resurrection panel is strikingly contemporary. He is completely free of skin lesions, and shows us only small scars where the nails had been placed in his hands and feet.[8] Most impressive of all in this panel, in terms of contemporary representational art, is the cosmic nature of Christ. Circular orbs of yellow surround him, blending into shades of orange, and a heavenly blue. This Christ is not only physically above the soldiers of the world, who are asleep on the ground, but is at one with the stars of the night sky. The circular light is otherworldly, meant, as in Suger's stained glass windows, to demonstrate that the divine light is of a different ontological order.

It is interesting to note that Grünewald placed the panel of resurrection adjacent to the nativity, with an exquisite Madonna and baby Jesus. Whereas Jesus' hands are wrenching in agony on the cross, Mary's, in contrast, are tenderly embracing her baby. Nevertheless, the face of resurrection is so human that one is startled by the gentle expression and soft smile of Jesus the Christ dressed in the powerful red robe of glory: the colossal sun glowing fecund in the red folds.

Giotto: Taking Us into the Reality of the Incarnation through Sight

Giotto di Bondone (ca. 1266–1337) gave to the world a new emphasis in painting: warm human emotion expressed through realism. Giotto was the son of a poor farmer. As a boy, while tending the sheep, Giotto would while away his time drawing on the rocks with a sharply pointed stone. This, claims Giorgio Vasari in his classic work *The Lives of the Artists*, is how the great Cimabue first saw the boy. According to Vasari's probably apocryphal story, Cimabue asked Giotto's father if the boy could come to Florence and be his apprentice.

Giotto's realistic foundation in nature ushered in a profound change in the pre-Renaissance period. Vasari credits him with having made a decisive break with the Byzantine style, with its stylized and elongated forms, and reintroducing a technique that had been neglected for more than two centuries, that of drawing accurately from life and thereby producing realistic three-dimensional figures.

For Giotto, the psychological reveals the spiritual. Devotional expressions, tears, joy, ecstasy, are important revealers of the spiritual state of the soul. Dante and Giotto were friends, and we cannot doubt the affinity between them—as Dante states in *Il Purgatorio*, "Cimabue thought to hold the field in painting, and now Giotto has the cry, so that the fame of the other is obscured."[9] Rachel Jacoff in *The Cambridge Companion to Dante* notes that when Dante met Giotto, Giotto was "at work in the Scrovegni Chapel—and one is left to imagine the exchanges between them."[10] Jacoff also notes that Dante's works were founded on contemplation: "Like Giotto's frescoes Dante had seen in Padua, all of which aim at inducing contemplation, his poem has its inevitable foundation in...contemplative theology."[11]

What makes Giotto so influential historically is the fact that his technical virtuosity found a counterpart in his profound spirituality. As with Dante, the eloquence of technical language, whether it be through word or paint, was inspired by spiritual truths.

Dante believed that the senses were the avenues to the mind and that sight was the most powerful ("noblest," he would have said) of these. Hence his art is predominantly visual.[12] Giotto, too, takes us into reality through sight. His fresco of Francis of Assisi recreating the nativity at Greccio is a moving example.

THE FIRST CRECHE AT GRECCIO

Francis wanted a new Bethlehem in Greccio; he prepared the setting to recreate the manger scene in every conceivable detail. According to the hagiography, at the moment Francis was to lift the Christ child from the crib the real Christ appeared as an infant. Giotto paints the scene with exquisite tenderness. The gaze between Francis and Christ is a glimpse beyond space and time, into the field of eternal unconditional love. This was Giotto's artistic revolution, portrayed in that gaze: the warmth, the exquisite tenderness, the almost excruciating vulnerability of spiritually bared souls. No ego, just Christ-consciousness, first at Greccio and then, in typical Franciscan emanation, penetrating into the world community.

Through his presence and single-minded devotion to Christ, Francis truly retrieved a Christ-centered spirituality that had been lost in the late medieval Church. Francis' love of all life, expressed in his kissing lepers, and his reverence toward all creation, was a song of mercy reflected in his living application of Matthew 25:40, "As you did it to one of the least of these you did it to me."

Giotto paints the gaze of human intimacy between Francis and the infant Jesus as a paragon of freeing love. He also paints, at Greccio, animals that show a feeling consciousness, a reality corroborated in scientific circles today but certainly not a part of medieval awareness. In this respect, too, Giotto was ahead of his time in his thinking.

Francis and Giotto represent a return to the Jesus of the Gospels. In large part, their return had to do with their grounding in creation—a love for and learning from nature. St. Francis' love of absolute poverty won for him a share in the wealth to which true, spiritual simplicity is the key. In the whole world he had nothing he could call his own; yet everything in the world seemed to belong to him through God, the Creator of the world. His attitude toward creation was simple and direct when he considered the universe in his pure, spiritual vision. Francis referred every created thing to the Creator of all. He saw God in everything, and loved and praised God in all creation. By God's generosity and goodness, Francis possessed God in everything, and everything in God. The realization that everything comes from the same source made Francis call all created things—no matter how insignificant—his brothers and sisters, because they had the same origin as he. However, he reserved his most tender compassion for those that are a natural reflection of Christ's gentleness and are used as figures of Jesus in Sacred Scripture.

So it was that by God's divine power the brute beasts felt drawn toward Francis and inanimate creation obeyed his will.

He was so united to all creation, so holy in his perceptions of Oneness, that he appeared to have returned to the state of primeval innocence.[13]

FRANCIS PREACHES TO THE BIRDS

Giotto portrays Francis in an attitude of humility. He is instructing the birds to quiet down so that he and another brother might pray the Divine Office. The birds had been so loud that the brothers could not hear themselves praying. Francis is the one who, while walking with this companion in the Venetian marshes, first hears the birds singing. He then says, "Our sisters the birds are praising their Creator. We will go in among them and sing God's praise, chanting the divine office."[14] But the birds are so loud that Francis has to preach to them: "My sisters, stop singing until we have given God the praise to which [God] has a right."[15]

For Francis, praying the Divine Office gave him a foundation, a structure, for his attitude toward the created world. Nature was glorious and was what the Franciscan theologian Bonaventure called "God's Book." However, humans also have minds that thirst for perspective and insight. *Lex orandi, lex credendi*: the way you pray determines the way you believe. Moreover, we need theological content to chew on and digest. Without content we might very well enter into the primal reality of nature, but we would not be fulfilling our total human potential, which includes intellectual insight as well. Francis was not one to emphasize the value of intellectual study and development, but many other saints, mystics, magicians, and theologians did, notably the Dominicans.

Lectio–Meditatio–Oratio–Contemplatio

Guigo II, the ninth prior of the Carthusian Order (ca.1173–1180) defines the medieval approach that influenced so many theologians and spiritual writers of the time: *lectio* (reading), *meditatio* (meditation), *oratio* (prayer), and *contemplatio* (contemplation).

In his *Ladder of Monks*, Guigo II made use of the image of the ladder from Jacob's dream in Genesis 28:12,[16] and "carefully constructed"[17] this short theological work, written as a letter-treatise.[18] From the extensive tradition of *lectio divina*, sacred reading, Guigo creates a solid prayerful system that begins with reading and culminates in profound mystical consciousness. Guigo is interested in individuals awakening their "interior senses," and in his schema, that awakening is only possible once one has integrated the first three steps of *lectio–meditatio–oratio* / reading–meditation–prayer.

Contemplatio is entrance into God-consciousness: "Contemplation is when the mind is in some sort lifted up to God and held above itself, so that it tastes the joy of everlasting sweetness...."[19] Consequently, one begins in the earthly realm of the mind, with reading, and finally enters heavenly secrets where one lets go of analytic rationality and enters into union with God.

Guigo repeatedly makes use of the word *sweetness* in his four ladder analogies:

> Reading seeks for the sweetness of the blessed life, meditation perceives it, prayer asks for it, contemplation tastes it. Reading, as it were, puts food whole into the mouth, meditation chews it and breaks it up, prayer extracts its flavor, and contemplation is sweetness itself which gladdens and refreshes.
>
> Reading works on the outside, meditation on the pith, prayer asks for what we long for, contemplation gives us delight in the sweetness we have found.[20]

Guigo continues in the *Ladder* analogously by describing the *lectio* Matthew 5:8:

"Blessed are the pure in heart, for they shall see God" as being placed in the soul's mouth; "like a page, biting and chewing it to stimulate reason to investigate the meaning of such purity on the anvil of meditation (*in incude meditationis*)."[21]

Guigo states that the verse itself is of great sweetness,[22] and only when we have bitten and chewed, stimulating reason and meditation, are we able to ask God in prayer for that ultimate sweetness—God's own presence and glory. *Contemplatio.*

Dame Julian

The English anchoress or hermit Julian of Norwich (1342–ca. 1416) left to Christian posterity what Harvey Egan calls "perhaps the most famous statement of Christian optimism in the entire (Christian) mystical tradition":[23]

> And so our good Lord answered to all the questions and doubts which I could raise, saying most comfortingly in this fashion: I will make all things well, I shall make all things well, I may make all things well, and I can make all things well; and you will see that yourself, that all things will be well.[24]

ALL THINGS WILL BE WELL

Julian had witnessed the historical realities of fourteenth-century England: "the epidemic and long-ranging effects of the Black Death, the Hundred Years' War, the Peasants' Revolt of 1381, the Lollard Controversy, the troubled reign of Richard II, the persecution of heresy throughout Europe, and the Great Schism."[25]

In her study of Julian as mystic and theologian, Grace Jantzen observes that when Julian speaks of the "great wretchedness of our mortal flesh,"[26] she is referring specifically to physical conditions and not making a moral or theological statement about the body. In other words, for Julian a "positive evaluation of the body" is an essential dimension of her *Summum Bonum*.[27] "What Julian is actually referring to is her own disease-wracked body and the miserable state to which we can be reduced by certain forms of disease."[28]

Jantzen makes the perceptive point that

> In modern times we are largely insulated from this unpleasantness. People suffering putrefying illnesses are hospitalized, and medical methods and modern sanitation do much to neutralize or at least camouflage the worst odors and protect us from the most distressing sights. But in days before antiseptics, and with poor sanitary arrangements, there must have been many instances of wounds which became infected and putrid, the sight and stench of which we can hardly imagine.[29]

Julian lived through the events of the fourteenth century and her own physical illness. Nevertheless, she still could "stand at the gates of doom" and "look through the gates of death" and yet declare: "All is included in [Christ]...the essential Mother, the real self, the very heaven. Nothing is lacking in him. Nothing can spoil or mutilate the perfection of all who are in All."[30]

Julian, the mystical theologian, could only make such statements because she faced the agonies of life unafraid, and by walking through that gate she entered the realm of the Eternal.

Here, in Christ-God, "all is well," and "all who are in the All" have passed through death into the arms of "the essential Mother, the real self, the very heaven."

THE MOTHERHOOD OF GOD

Dame Julian developed a theology of Christ as God our mother, "which had a long tradition, but she brought it to a height of theological sophistication beyond anything found in earlier literature."[31] Julian declares, "In essence motherhood means love and kindness, wisdom, knowledge, goodness."[32] Julian brings a warm relational face to the godhead, which is not always true of mystics' descriptions of the Divine, and she presents us with a God that she describes with feminine imagery. She gives us a God who is Mother, tenderly caring for us as if we were a tiny, fragile hazelnut:

> I looked at the hazel nut with the eye of my understanding and thought, what can this be? I was amazed that it could last for I thought that because of its littleness it would suddenly have fallen into nothing. And I was answered in my understanding. It lasts and always will, because God loves it, and thus everything has being through the love of God.[33]

ENDLESS BLISS

For Julian, Christ gives us the "inner certainty of endless bliss."[34] Why? Because no matter the vicissitudes of life, Christ our Mother "most tenderly" loves us:[35] "The mother can lay her child tenderly to her breast, but our tender Mother Jesus can lead us easily into his blessed breast through his open side, and show us there a part of the godhead and of the joys of heaven, with inner certainty of endless bliss."[36] This showing ends with Julian's well-known statement that "love was his meaning."[37]

Julian then discloses that she did not fully understand the revelation at the time but, after many years, she received her answer:

> What, do you wish to know our Lord's meaning in this thing? Know it well, love was his meaning. Who reveals it to you? Love. What did he reveal to you? Love. Why does he reveal it to you? For love. Remain in this, and you will know more of the same. But you will never know different, without end.[38]

From the commonplace image of the hazelnut, Julian takes us right into the open side of Christ, where we are shown a part of the eternal, invisible godhead and the joys of heaven. God is love since God is the "eternal satisfaction of every genuine desire."[39] God is love itself anthropomorphically imaged by Julian as Mother and Father. "God is as really our Mother as he is our Father...I who am Unity."[40]

Julian is a true medieval representative as she maintains her vision of union with God as an ever-present reality. Union with God permeated medieval life, art, and spirituality, and Julian describes one way to get there.

We have examined the foundation and symbolism of cathedral theology, the work of such artists as Matthias Grünewald, and the prayerful inspiration of *Lectio–Meditatio–Oratio–Contemplatio*. We can see that these "guides" are still important today. In fact, the theology and visions of medieval tradition and culture help us in today's secular society to maintain a spiritual life by embarking on an internal pilgrimage beyond the limits of time.

Chapter 2

THE REAL WORLD IS INSIDE: TERESA OF AVILA

Teresa of Avila began to write her *Interior Castle* when she was sixty-two years old. Teresa was not loved by everyone in her own lifetime; in fact, at sixty-two she was being investigated by the Inquisition, and when her own nuns voted once more to have Teresa as their Prioress, they were excommunicated. Eventually, this situation was rectified; however, as with other misrepresentations in her life, Teresa clearly saw the injustice and wrote that the situation "was so offensive to everyone."[1]

Teresa suffered from poor health, harsh living conditions, and unfair treatment. Still, her sisters knew her as a woman of humor, levelheaded, and a model of contemplative prayer. She began *The Interior Castle* on June 2, 1577, with the goal of describing as lucidly as possible the interior dwelling places of the psyche. One of her nuns, Mother Maria del Nacimiento, wrote a deposition describing Saint Teresa as she composed *The Interior Castle*. It is one of the only descriptions we have:

> When the said Mother Teresa of Jesus wrote the book called *The Dwelling Places*, she was in Toledo, and this witness saw that it was after communion that she wrote this book, and when she wrote she did so very rapidly and with such great beauty in her countenance that this witness was in admiration, and she was so

17

absorbed in what she was writing that even if some noise was made there, it did not hinder her; wherefore this witness understood that in all that she wrote and during the time she was writing she was in prayer.[2]

Fig. 2: Gian Lorenzo Bernini (1598–1680), *The Ecstasy of Saint Teresa* (close-up).

Teresa had reached the heights of the mystical life (see fig. 2). What Maria del Nacimiento refers to as *The Dwelling Places* became known as *The Interior Castle*, and it is into this that Teresa leads us. Teresa's concentration during prayer was one of the most significant practices for entering the spiritual life and for the interior journey to the profoundest depths of prayer and union with God.

Teresa was a spiritual lioness. She was humble and loving, but too true to the Divine within to be obsequious. Teresa's lioness-nature enabled her to handle the Inquisition. She developed spiritually because she heard God's voice in prayer. Like Joan of Arc, that voice made demands that only a woman with a strong image of herself as, for example, a knight, could fulfill.

GIVING TIME

We sometimes tend to believe that God will take care of everything, and that we do not have to devote scheduled time to maintaining our relationship with God. We take God for granted and do not give that God-conscious relationship the time we would give to our intimate human circle of family and friends.

If we did give God time, this would lead us to want to give God more time. Time with God nourishes and regenerates our deepest center. When we are "united with the Strong One through so sovereign a union of spirit with spirit...,"[3] we are guided by the spirit and live through the spirit. We become increasingly fearless, happier, and liberated. The process is similar to that of practicing the piano. Sometimes even the most tedious practice sessions lead to a relational oneness with the music, in which all the elements, from the staccato notes to the sustained phrasing, eventually flow into a musical unity.

PRACTICE

Teresa wrote that "obedience usually lessens the difficulty of things that seem impossible."[4] In one way, she was blessed to be living at a time in history when obedience to God was valued. For one to say that they needed time to be with God would be acceptable, and most likely, admired. Teresa persevered in prayer as her path in life to concentrate on deepening her relationship with God. Much of Teresa's strength and humility arose from her experience of God's presence in prayer. In this way she developed the spiritual qualities that enabled her to persist through the changes, the joys, and sorrows of life.

Teresa believed that obedience consisted in listening to the voice of God within and in following the guidance of the Holy Spirit. Obedience defined her life and identity: to disobey God's will was to face the loss of God's presence. Nothing was worth the absence of God in Teresa's daily existence. The older Teresa became, the more she wanted to maintain a state of union with God. Thus she came to value obedience as a direct means of persevering in the spiritual life. She explains the process of spiritual development and union with God in *The Interior Castle*.

THE INTERIOR CASTLE

The image of the castle is magnificent. The castle is the Self and Christ reigns at its center. The castle is a *mandala*, Sanskrit for circle, and one of those powerful archetypal images that help us integrate realities too subtle and difficult to reach through normal consciousness. A dream about our home or a house may have to do with the structure of our Self and our identity.

For Teresa, Christ is the goal and model of the Self. Christ, through his example, shows us God. By becoming increasingly God-conscious, we come closer to the Christ within. Teresa tells us that the Christ within may be covered over with the grime of the ego, so much so that we have lost contact with our deepest interior. We have to penetrate, she says, into "the extreme interior...very deep within [to] experience the divine."[5] It is only through these experiences of God that we become able to recognize the difference between our true self and our ego projections.

Teresa was wise enough to know that mind experiences need to be tested and shared with others. She advised her sisters to be honest with their spiritual directors. She knew that the mind can play tricks on us, but she had the insight to know that no trick of the mind could replicate the presence of God, and that eventually, if the experience was of God within, that tender and strong presence would lead to a "happy peace."[6]

SEVEN DWELLING PLACES

Teresa's castle of the Divine Self has seven dwelling places. The castle is crystalline, beautiful, and transparent. If we come to know the Self, we know who we are and we understand the interior design of our motivations and involvements. This may take a lifetime, but for Teresa, that is our meaning in life and the spiritual journey.

To come to understand the seven dwelling places is to discover our spiritual Self. For Teresa, "The brilliance of this inner vision is like that of an infused light coming from a sun covered by something as transparent as a properly-cut diamond. The garment seems made of a fine Dutch linen."[7]

Once we have encountered the infused light, we never want to be far in thought or action from the presence of God. We recognize the difference between acting from the ego and being centered in the divine castle within, our true home.

THE CASTLE AS AWARENESS

Hence, the Teresian castle is God-consciousness and the seven dwelling places are evolving levels of awareness. If we reach the apex, we experience the bliss of crystalline liberation within and a spiritual marriage with the presence of God: "A person walks in an admirable way with Christ…in whom the divine and human are joined and who is always that person's companion."[8]

For Teresa, this is not an escape but a life joining the fully divine and fully human in compassionate service, fulfilling one's divinely given individual gifts. These gifts, whether they are literary, or athletic, in parenting, teaching, or scientific inquiry, are blessings to be shared.

As we evolve in consciousness, the lower dwelling of ignorance, mediocrity, and ego protection has less power to deceive us. We become wise to our own interior antics, neuroses, petty thoughts, and behaviors, in order "not to be like dunces, wasting time."[9] We accept our divine gifts and share them through our humanity, just as Christ modeled the way to live continuously in the presence of God.

The castle is a metaphor of wakefulness. We may remain asleep in a specific dwelling of the castle, a metaphor for a fear or habit that we are unwilling to overcome.

The person who walks the castle hallways meets shadows in the dark as well as surprising insights. Teresa tells us that we may enter through the gate of prayer, because part of accepting the invitation into the castle is to accept the mystery of God at the center.

THE FIRST DWELLING

Our guide is the "good Jesus"[10] and Teresa tells us in the First Dwelling that we are made in God's image, although it is "almost impossible for us to understand the sublime dignity and beauty of the soul."[11] Sin clouds our understanding, as does the fact that we are not raised to appreciate our divine nature and human gifts.

In any case, the First Dwelling demonstrates what lies outside the beauty and dignity of the castle wall of the Self, and it is not a pretty sight.

> It is a shame and unfortunate that through our own fault we don't understand ourselves or know who we are. Wouldn't it show great ignorance, my daughters, if someone when asked who he was didn't know, and didn't know his father or mother or from what country he came? Well now, if this would be so extremely stupid, we are incomparably more so when we do not strive to know who we are....
>
> We seldom consider the precious things that can be found in this soul, or who dwells within it, or its high

value. Consequently, little effort is taken up with the plainness of the diamond's setting or the outer wall of the castle.[12]

We don't like being called "stupid," but Teresa uses these words about herself first. We might prefer other words, like "ignorant" or "conditioned," but let us not lose sight of the fact that her language jolts us into an uncomfortable awareness.

The Outer Courtyard. Who are the guards at the castle's outer walls? Saint Teresa identifies them as the vermin and insects of our negative mental habits and warns that we can become accustomed to them. Indeed, we may not want to proceed beyond the outer walls. Yet even when we are trapped in this state of negativity, we still have "so rich a nature and power to converse with none other than God."[13]

The problem is that we may not want to change; we may not wish to acknowledge our rich potential. If we do not make the internal commitment to change, we are stuck in our misery. A certain "learned man," Teresa tells us, described people who actually decide not to change as paralyzed spiritually. Some scholars think this "learned man" is Saint John of the Cross, who was her spiritual director from 1575–1577, and with whom she enjoyed one of the most profound friendships in history.[14]

Need for Reflection. Teresa next tells us that prayer needs to be reflective. Without understanding or insight, vocal prayer does not lead us into the castle of the Self. Therefore, in the very beginning of the journey into the castle, we need to be attentive to our thoughts. This idea is in the majority of world religions and is the difference between lip-service religiosity—what Jean-Paul Sartre called "bad faith"—and authentic spirituality. We must understand why we are praying and where we hope to proceed in our relationship to God.

Teresa gives examples of people in different internal perceptual states. In the First Dwelling, those who enter only briefly bring reptiles into the castle. Their ultimate treasure is not a commitment to understanding, but distractions. They take a little time to enter but cannot fully enjoy the fountains, gardens, and center of the castle, because other parts of their lives call them away from self-understanding.[15]

The Tree of Life. The Interior Castle is lush with archetypal imagery. One of these archetypes is that of the Tree of Life. If we plant ourselves in the fountain of life—God-consciousness—the grace of God nourishes us and we bear fruit. If we plant ourselves in darkness, away from the castle, we are exercising "bad management"[16] and live in wretchedness.

The term *bad management* is worth mentioning because it indicates that taking care of ourselves spiritually needs organization. In our contemporary world we are advised to schedule time for prayer or exercise and to put it on the calendar. Otherwise we will not give prayer or exercise the commitment that we would give, for example, to a business appointment. Teresa understood the importance of managing one's priorities and the destructive possibilities that could ensue if we neglect our own personal organization.

We could carry the image of the Tree of Life further and say that if we plant a tree to enhance and manage the castle, we are nourished by the life of the castle. This tree would add beauty, shade, and fruit. If we plant our tree away from the castle, where there is no light and clear water, our tree eventually dies. We are unable to reflect positively on consciousness; we are instead chaos, fear, and death.

The Second Dwelling. In the Second Dwelling Teresa accentuates the theme of conformity to the will of God. Once we enter the castle we are drawn by the outside distractions unless we conform to God's will.

How do we recognize God's will in our life? Through detachment and listening to the way events unfold in our lives. The Spirit works through situations; if we do not learn to listen to spontaneous direction and seemingly random events, we may very well miss the guidance of the Spirit.

The temptations outside the castle have little or nothing to do with the life in the Spirit, with conformity to God's will. When we are drawn back out of the castle we settle for distractions that do not give us the interior freedom and happy peace of life in the castle. "Can there be an evil greater than that of being ill at ease in our own house? What hope can we have of finding rest outside ourselves if we cannot be at rest within?"[17]

The War Within. Teresa's language is decisive. Like a good number of mystics, she identifies inner peace with living in the Spirit and a good life. If we are ill at ease in ourselves, we may seek diversion, but we are not working from the center of the Self, the castle, our ontological home.

War, anger, hatred, violence, and fighting take us away from the castle. You can feel the alienation; it is a palpable pull away from center. "Well, believe me, if we don't have peace within our own house we'll not find it outside. Let this war be ended."[18]

Why Peace Is Exciting. Peace within is exciting because we become conscious of God's presence and guidance. We are at home in the universe. We are not separate from the world, from our bodies, from nature: We are one. The vast mystery of life opens to us and we answer through even our ordinary actions.

The gift of a simplified life is experiencing infinity in a grain of sand. All the noise and consumer distractions pale next to the peaceful presence of mystery. It takes an evolved consciousness to recognize the difference between the stimulation of contrived reactions and sensations, and what Teresa calls nakedness and detachment—an ability to stand with an open soul and experience, moment-by-moment, immeasurable glory.

THE THIRD DWELLING

"Enter, enter, my daughters, into the interior rooms."[19] Out of the awareness of interiority comes the immeasurable glory of resting in the presence of God.

In the Third Dwelling Teresa warns that if we judge others, we may miss the mark. It takes our time and energy to look at and analyze other people's behavior; better to scrutinize ourselves and ensure that we are aligned with God's will.

"Doing our own will is what usually harms us."[20] Hence, by being conscious of our own obedience, that is, awareness of resting in the Spirit, we come to live in the castle of presence more confidently.

How do we discern the difference between our own will and God's will? Many religious thinkers and mystics have addressed this question. Spiritual discernment takes time to develop. There are tests to help us develop discernment. Certainly one of the great Christian writers on discernment is Ignatius of Loyola.

Briefly, discernment means to try to analyze whether what we want is in line with God's will, the way the Spirit is moving in our life. Can we can stand back from the results and be at peace? If, on the other hand, we feel a need to determine the outcome, the desire may be more our own ego motivation than where the Spirit is leading us.

THE FOURTH DWELLING

Discernment is a habit, a manageable habit. One of Teresa's gifts is that she makes manageable and almost ordinary what can be regarded as esoteric. She has no pretenses. What she describes as leading to the heights of mystical awareness is accessible if we prioritize our relationship with God and manage our time in order to do so. Teresa writes in the Fourth Dwelling that this habit is "difficult to acquire" and therefore "we may not manage to remain inside" the castle.[21] We have walked "in the environs of the castle,"[22] but we cannot stay there because we have not been willing to make it a habit.

Once we base our life on "an excellent kind of meditation... which is that God is within us,"[23] we really have given ourselves the greatest gift in terms of self-regard, an acknowledgement that we are worth the time it takes to meditate on the reality of God within us.

Suffering. In the Fourth Dwelling Teresa states that we cause much of our own suffering.[24] "For the most part," she says, "all the trials and disturbances come from our not understanding ourselves."[25] If we come to understand ourselves more deeply, we recover our soul and become "attentive to interior matters."[26]

Much suffering is reactive. If we could detach ourselves sufficiently to look at our involvements and choose as much as possible whom to be with, what to do, how to do it, and how much time and energy to give, we would be united more closely with the Spirit and would free ourselves from much needless suffering.

In God's Hands. Once we develop the habit of prayer, we can live in a state in which we allow ourselves to let go. Our minds do not ramble as much; we have become more accustomed to resting in meditation. If we do begin something, we know enough to surrender it to God, placing it in the loving hands of the Spirit.

We cannot know how any particular problem will be solved. We can know that if we let it go and give the Spirit time, having the patience to wait in trust, an outcome greater than what we could have wrought will indeed result. We just have to remember to let go, especially when it is a dilemma that is especially worrisome, such as a health concern or an issue involving someone we love.

Prayer of Quiet. Teresa calls recollection the prayer of quiet and compares it to water in a large trough in which the water does not overflow, but quietly fills the space within with sweetness. In the Fourth Dwelling Teresa uses another metaphor, that of a child suckling at his or her mother's breasts. In either of these metaphors, we can sense the quiet contentment, the ability not to react and rush, the willingness to let water and nourishment fill our being.

THE FIFTH DWELLING

In the Fifth Dwelling, we rest so completely in God that Teresa compares this state of meditation to a worm in the cocoon of Christ. The worm is protected by Christ's spirit, slowly metamorphosing into the Spirit itself just as the worm changes into a lovely white butterfly.

> Now, then, let's see what this silkworm does, for that's the reason I've said everything else. When the soul is, in this prayer, truly dead to the world, a little white butterfly comes forth. Oh, greatness of God! How transformed the soul is when it comes out of this prayer after having been placed in the greatness of God and so closely joined with Him for a little while....Truly, I tell you, that the soul doesn't recognize itself. Look at the difference there is between an ugly worm and a little white butterfly; that's what the difference is here.[27]

Ordinary Worm, Ordinary Butterfly. Whether an ordinary ugly worm or an ordinary white butterfly results, the sacred transformation Teresa describes is still in the ordinary, natural realm. That is, the "doing" butterfly, the little white butterfly of action, is transformed through the contemplative time it has spent with God. Protected and nourished by the cocoon of meditation, the worm that thought it was ugly begins to be transformed into the butterfly it was meant to be.

Although these analogies seem strained and confusing at times, Teresa's use of them is necessary. If we remained in a meditative state aware of the presence of God within and without, we would not need the image of the ugly worm. But because we allow ourselves to become ugly by removing ourselves from the cocoon of protective divine care, we need an image to help us restore ourselves to what Buddhism calls our original nature.

Original Nature. We have never been separated from our original nature; nevertheless, because we believe the deception of duality, our *doing* self and our *being* selves are not harmoniously synchronized.

The music of the Sacred Self is harmony. Our original nature is not disjointed or alienated. Teresa is referring to a state described in the book of Genesis as being made in the image and likeness of God.

Teresa employs the images of an ugly worm and a little butterfly to point out that we are not both ego and sacred nature. She states that we cannot easily retreat from this state. Once we have opened ourselves to union with God, ordinary awareness is much more satisfying than the diversions of the artificial ego.

THE SIXTH DWELLING

The Sixth and Seventh Dwellings are not that distinct from each other. In the Sixth Dwelling, the presence of Christ in everything becomes a constant in one's life. There is no strain or separation of consciousness. Self-knowledge and truth become one.

Teresa has been referred to as a psychological mystic, and in the Sixth Dwelling we can see why. She describes self-knowledge as sometimes painful but always necessary. Not to remain in self-understanding is to lose God. Teresa's groundedness comes from the fact that the deepest insight into our own denials, flaws, and motives, both positive and negative, brings us into the center of the castle.

Truth and Wakefulness. We can equate truth with spiritual wakefulness. That means that when Teresa tells us always to remain truthful, we would therein remain spiritually awake. "Thus, we shall have little esteem for this world, which is a complete lie and falsehood...."[28] It might seem extreme to assert that the world is a complete lie and falsehood; however, we can say that unless we stay awake and are truthful about ourselves and the human condition, we enter into a collective lie that deceives us in terms of what the world is ontologically.

Is the world culturally determined, or is there a deeper spiritual truth to which Teresa is referring? Let's use an example like advertising.

A cultural lie fostered by our society is something against which, in Teresa's definition, we have to fight diligently. The importance of owning a new car, being thin, or using a certain detergent, are contemporary lies that thousands of people literally buy into, and willingly at that.

Teresa asks, "are you able to drink the chalice?"[29] In other words, can you take the discomfort, perhaps the hostility of not going along with a collective lie? Subsequently she says that we would "answer yes; and very rightly so"[30] at the center of the Self. She has so much confidence in God that she ends the Sixth Dwelling by telling us that God will give us strength and actually defends "these souls in all things; when they are persecuted and criticized."[31]

THE SEVENTH DWELLING

In the Seventh Dwelling we are joined to the uncreated Spirit of the universe.[32] We are no longer separate from Christ; our life is now Christ.[33] Teresa uses metaphors to describe this spiritual union:

> The soul always remains with God in that center....In the spiritual marriage the union is like what we have when rain falls from the sky into a river or fount; all is water, for the rain that fell from heaven cannot be divided or separated from the water of the river. Or it is like what we have when a little stream enters the sea, there is no means of separating the two. Or, like the bright light entering a room through two different windows; although the streams of light are separate when entering the room, they become one.[34]

What happens in the person who is at one with God, the uncreated Spirit of the universe? Bliss. All the troubles in the Sixth Dwelling that are inherent in being truthful about personal and collective lies disappear in the bliss of the Seventh Dwelling. Teresa knew the lives of the saints and recognized throughout *The Interior Castle* that even in times of trouble, one could still be at peace within oneself.

Deepest Silence. The happy peace of the Seventh Dwelling is found in the "deepest silence."[35] One is amazed, but it is an awe and amazement that is like a quiet, knowing smile.

In Mahayana Buddhism a Bodhisattva (*Bodhi* = wisdom, *sattva* = being) is one who, after achieving enlightenment, does not disappear into nirvana, but rather comes back to teach humanity the way to liberation. The quietness Teresa describes is much like the Bodhisattva's smile in Chinese art.[36] She hears the cries of the world and gracefully responds with the message of compassionate wisdom and internal freedom.

Finally, Teresa tells us to love and do good works, not to "build castles in the air."[37] By loving we share all we have learned as to the benefits of castle living, dwelling in oneness with God, and appreciating the true gifts of life in this world.

Once we have found peace in the castle, no one can take it from us; we are at rest, energized and made whole within.

Chapter 3

THE JEWISH MYSTICAL VIEW: THE KABBALAH

Jewish mysticism had its own banquet of rich delights in the medieval period. This can seem amazing when one considers the historical plight of the persecuted Jews in a politically Christian European empire. And yet, Judaism had its own abundant tradition of spirituality, a fact that was repeatedly ignored by Christians.

The *Zohar* and the *Sefirot*

In the thirteenth century Moses de León, a Jewish mystic in Spain, published a work known as the *Zohar*. Moses de León attributed its authorship to "the...teacher Shim'on bar Yohai [sometimes referred to as Simeon Bar Yochai], whose ancient authority sanctioned the publication of the secrets."[1] Rabbi Simeon Bar Yochai is believed to have been a Palestinian Jewish teacher who lived in the second century.[2] More recent scholarship believes that Moses de León himself wrote the book. The Zohar is the canonical text of the Kabbalah. It is based on the Talmud, early Jewish mystical works, and various *midrashim*, as well as on the scripture commentaries of various medieval rabbis. The Kabbalists mined the Hebrew Scriptures for mystical symbols that they believed to be of divine origin since Scripture was divinely inspired, and the Zohar shows the influence of this.

The word *Zohar* is translated as "splendor" or "illumination." The illumination of our minds with the knowledge of God takes place through the *sefirot*, or ten energies of God (see fig. 3), which emanate from the *Ein Sof*, the boundless, invisible, spiritual realm of Divine Unity.[3] Moses de Leon describes the sefirot in the Zohar. There is no form materially able to reveal fully the Transcendent God.[4] The sefirot reveal God's being to our minds.

The word *sefirot* originally meant "numerals" (the singular is *sefirah*). It expresses the belief that the aspects of God's being or instruments of God's activity can be counted. Some Kabbalists also say that the word comes from the Hebrew word *sapper*, which means to tell—thus the sefirot tell us about God.[5] A similar relationship between "count" and "tell" exists in the English and other languages: think, for example, of the interchangeable expressions for praying the rosary, "counting one's beads" and "telling one's beads." Some Kabbalists claim that *sefirot* comes from the Hebrew word for sapphire. Like a radiant gem, the sefirot illumine our knowledge of God.

The sefirot are envisioned as an upside down tree with ten roots in God's very Being. The roots, are, therefore, nourished in the spiritual realm as the tree grows into the world of matter. If we as spiritual beings keep our roots in the invisible realm, we are fulfilling our spiritual destiny. There is also a parallel between the sefirot and the Hindu *chakras*, in that both are imaged as a map corresponding to specific areas of the human body that have symbolic significance.

The First Sefirah: *Keter*, the Crown

The first sefirah is *Keter*, the Crown. "So closely united with '*Ein Sof* is *Keter* that many regarded it to be as much a part of the concealed God as it is an actual emanation from '*Ein Sof*."[6] For

Fig. 3: *The Ten Sefirot.*

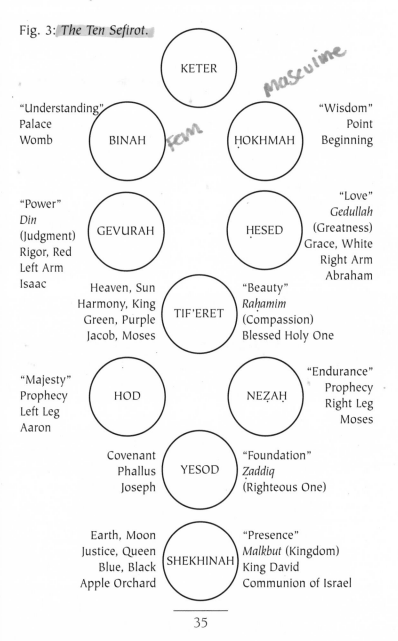

KETER

Masculine

Fem

"Understanding"
Palace
Womb

BINAH

"Wisdom"
Point
Beginning

HOKHMAH

"Power"
Din
(Judgment)
Rigor, Red
Left Arm
Isaac

GEVURAH

"Love"
Gedullah
(Greatness)
Grace, White
Right Arm
Abraham

HESED

Heaven, Sun
Harmony, King
Green, Purple
Jacob, Moses

TIF'ERET

"Beauty"
Rahamim
(Compassion)
Blessed Holy One

"Majesty"
Prophecy
Left Leg
Aaron

HOD

"Endurance"
Prophecy
Right Leg
Moses

NEZAH

Covenant
Phallus
Joseph

YESOD

"Foundation"
Zaddiq
(Righteous One)

Earth, Moon
Justice, Queen
Blue, Black
Apple Orchard

SHEKHINAH

"Presence"
Malkbut (Kingdom)
King David
Communion of Israel

that reason, the Crown inspires the creation of matter. In other words, the Crown of the revealing sefirot makes visible the invisible Divine.

God's Being is our nourishment. Keter, as the crown of our spiritual identity, is Primal Will. If this sounds Neoplatonic, remember that many elements of the sefirot are derived from Neoplatonism, such as the image of radiating light emanating from the Godhead.[7] While the Neoplatonic system of emanations is static and fixed, however, the sefirot are dynamic, "constantly moving in a rhythm of change."[8] The hidden Godhead itself does not move or change, "thus resembling to some extent the Aristotelian concept of the Prime Mover or First Cause."[9] Keter is "the point beyond which the imagination cannot penetrate."[10] To rise into Keter through spiritual experience is to begin to emerge into comprehending the ten sefirot. In Christian terms, Thomas Merton called such a process "a raid on the unspeakable."

In my new course on great mystics of the world, Keter was difficult for us to understand when we studied our section on Jewish mysticism. If we are in a situation where all our thoughts are stilled, empty of positing goals or rehashing scenarios, we touch Keter.

Ultimately, one must enter this realm and go into the dark reaches of inner space. In Kabbalistic tradition, one undertook these kinds of investigations after one's fortieth birthday. Only then was one able to enter the doors of perception demanding that the normal modes of consciousness with which one usually prayed be left at the gate. Before the age of forty, one was thought, rightfully in Jewish tradition, to be too involved physiologically and psychologically in the basics of life such as marital, familial, and financial obligations.

After forty, when life's necessities are not as demanding, one may enter the doors of perception. Let us read these words from the Kabbalah:

The depth of primordial being is called Boundless. Because of its concealment from all creatures above and below, it is also called Nothingness. If one asks, "What is it?" the answer is, "Nothing," meaning: No one can understand anything about it. It is negated of every conception. No one can know anything about it—except the belief that it exists. Its existence cannot be grasped by anyone other than it. Therefore its name is "I am becoming."[11]

"I am becoming" is the participation we have in Nothingness becoming Being. The philosophical depth of the Kabbalah is evident here. There is no compromise with the Transcendent God; we simply cannot grasp it since it negates every concept. We can, however, have faith as a bridge into the Ultimate Mystery.

Why is it so important to acknowledge God's transcendence? Because if we attempt to categorize God, we lose the internal purity of mind wherein contact with divine Being can indeed take place experientially.

This is a psychological insight into how the mind works; if we posit any kind of philosophical or theological concept, we latch onto that theory and can no longer be open to the Mystery of the universe. "The essence of faith is an awareness of the vastness of Infinity."[12]

The Second and Third Sefirot:
Hokhmah and *Binah*,
Wisdom and Intelligence

Keter still bridges two "worlds," simultaneously resting in God's concealment and positing the Divine into the distinct sefirot. It is only with the second sefirah, *Hokhmah* or wisdom, "that we can speak of actual 'thingness' or existence within the sefirotic structure."[13]

Hokhmah, interestingly, is the first discernable aspect of God, the Beginning, the primordial point—that is, our contact point between Divine Mind and our inner ability to begin to discern transcendence.

Can we discern here the human quality of developed wisdom? Not just intelligence, but the integration of intuition and intelligence through experiential reflection. Wisdom is that which we know and comprehend through experience:

> When you train yourself to hear the voice of God in everything, you attain the quintessence of the human spirit. Usually the mind conceals the divine thoroughly by imagining that there is a separate mental power that constructs the mental images. But by training yourself to hear the voice of God in everything, the voice reveals itself to your mind as well. Then right in the mind, you discover revelation.[14]

The expression "Then right in the mind" is wonderful. To be in one's right mind is the mind without bad habits, mental projections, even theological concepts about God. A mind that is not right is a mind that is not open to divine transcendence. That openness is the beginning of wisdom because it is a humble acknowledgement of our human limitations in the face of the Ultimate Transcendence of the invisible God.

God is in everything. How can we know and experience the sacred in all our life situations? "Train yourself to eliminate negative habits such as anger, depression, impatience, and chatter."[15]

Unlike many other mystical systems, Hokhmah, wisdom, is imaged in the Zohar as the active masculine principle within

God.[16] Hokhmah impregnates *Binah*, intelligence, the third sefi-rah.[17] Hence, Hokhmah is the upper Father of the sefirot, and Binah is the upper Mother.

Binah is the womb, the divine Mother who births the "chil-dren" of the lower seven sefirot.[18] Binah is also called the Building or Palace that contains the rooms of the lower sefirot.

In other words, the living God is discovered through the "infinite abundance of images and symbols, each relating to a particular aspect of God."[19] And the particular aspects of God reveal the teaching of Genesis: to make human beings in God's image after the divine likeness.[20]

The spiritual journey individually and internally is the same process for the Kabbalists that took place cosmically in Genesis.

When we come to Hokhmah and Binah, that unity of wis-dom and intelligence, we discover clearly what the Kabbalists are seeking, namely that "he or she is not exploring something 'up there,' but rather the beyond that lies within."[21] Hence, the tree of the sefirot is descriptive of an internal landscape and how we connect to God through spiritual experience and insight.

The Fourth and Fifth Sefirot: *Hesed* and *Gevurah*, Love and Power

The fourth sefirah, *Hesed* or love, is bonded to the fifth, *Gevurah* or power. Love without justice is ineffectual and justice without mercy can be heartless and cruel.

Love needs the left arm of power and rationality. Power needs the right arm of tempering love and energy. Once one integrates the sefirot, the rational dimension of oneself and the motivational energy of love keep each other in check through a continuing tension of complementarity.

The metaphor of a human body would have Hesed and Gevurah as the arms. Love and Power balance each other. Just as an obvious imbalance would occur if one arm was longer than the other arm, so it is with Hesed and Gevurah. In our Great Mystics class we discussed "soft love," that is, love without power. Soft love can be destructive even though the person tremendously loves and may have good intentions.

The Sixth Sefirah: *Tif'eret*, Beauty

Beauty is the trunk of the cosmic tree, the sixth sefirah, *Tif'eret.* When one unites love and power, one is beautiful. The beauty of the divine in the human sphere is the integration of power and love. When we read a beautiful novel, or see a beautiful film, that novel or film integrates love and power. When we view a beautiful film, for example, it combines the believable Power of the acting, the intensity of the music, the directorial choice of frames and pace of the images, with the director's committed Love for the actor's capability and the setting's mood. The film may be on an "ugly" topic such as war, but if that theme is expressed artistically, a beautiful movie has been created. *The Two Towers* of the *Lord of the Rings* films is medievalesque and gruesome; yet, it is a beautiful film. The depiction of the battle royale for forty minutes had me riveted in my seat, because one could feel the play of good against evil. A truly ethical act may be beautiful.

Societal definitions of beauty are extremely limited. Attitudes toward physical beauty are changing, but we have a long way to go as a culture. Is there a human face that is not beautiful? In Japanese haiku, wrinkles, individual smiles, eye color and shape, different noses and facial color—all are beautiful, revealing the sacred.

For the Kabbalists, beauty as Tif'eret is the characteristic of harmony. If I put someone else's eyes on my face, the harmony of my own facial features would be lost. If only one facial structure or color is thought socially to be attractive, we have forfeited the vast panoply of ethnic variety.

Tif'eret gives stability through harmony. I am free to love myself as I love the beauty of my individuality. Freedom is the comfort I feel within my own skin. How many of us, both male and female, especially as teenagers, have not been self-conscious about not meeting the media's stifling ideas of attractiveness (I refuse to say beauty!)? Almost all of us, sadly.

To be one in Tif'eret is to recognize the harmony of the divinely revealed beauty in one's own "image and likeness" to God. From the perspective of Tif'eret, we could say that it is insulting to God not to like our own appearance. This might help us to think deeply about, for instance, placing foreign plastic implants in female or male chests,[22] and to consider with spiritual detachment and Tif'eret values the health costs, the financial cost, and the psychological statement we are making to ourselves about who we are physically and what place those choices have in our identity as a human being.

We have not even touched on the infinite visible examples of Beauty around us in the natural world. Every tree, butterfly, dog's face reflects Beauty to us. If we were stable in Tif'eret, we would live more mindfully because we would be taken into the sacred appreciation of the moment surrounding us.

Each sefirah calls on us to do our part in terms of coming into relationship with God. The sefirot of God make our lives holy in large part because we are willing to give our time to the blessings that rain down upon us through life's most ordinary happenings.

The Seventh and Eighth Sefirot: *Netsah* and *Hod*, Eternity and Splendor

The seventh sefirah, *Netsah*, eternity, symbolizes the endurance of God. Netsah is partnered with the eighth, *Hod*, splendor, as the legs of the sefirot. God's splendor is mysterious and the source of prophecy.

Eternity and splendor keep us centered in God. If we can consciously do what we have to do, we are living now in the splendor of eternity. For the sefirot, if we abandon Netsah and Hod, we will live in chaos. Why? Because human beings are made in the image and likeness of God. If we forget and neglect this fact, our eternal splendorous nature, we live in chaos.

Netsah, eternity, and Hod, splendor, are the earth without exploitive power. When evil not only tortures, but kills the green of life, we witness the purposeless of evil. The splendor of God obvious in trees and living ecosystems is replaced by metal and death.

At least in most of our lives, evil does not come in such dramatic contrasts. It may be true that we are committed to political values represented in respecting life and ecosystems. Much of what we encounter on a daily basis, however, is not overtly good or evil. By meditating on eternity and splendor, we become more sensitized to our own perceptions and life. How many of our decisions revolve around a dilemma, for example?—dilemmas that are not especially good or evil, but multilayered and complex.

The Ninth and Tenth Sefirot: *Yesod* and *Shekhinah*, the Male and Female Principles

Netzah and Hod are the bliss of the sacred. That bliss may be God's presence in music, in nature, in relaxing conversationally with a friend. If we lose the closeness of eternal splendor, we lose the divine order that holds our universe together. I think that is why Tolkien has the Hobbits love ordinary life so much, eating, celebrating, and cultivating with care their plentiful gardens.

The bliss of the sacred establishes our being in the energy of God. That energy is *Yesod*, the generative phallus (in an anthropomorphic sense) and the ninth sefirah. Yesod is united to *Shekhinah*, the feminine presence of God's glory and the tenth sefirah. These two are paired as the link between the divine and the more secularized world.

Yesod and Shekhinah is a bond between God and God's people. If we stay in touch with the generative energy of God aware of God's presence, we may be in the world but not of it. We are not metaphysical-spiritual beings only as we come to embody the characteristics of God in the sefirot. Rather, we join with the rest of the world as one earthly community united in our divine potentiality through the presence of Shekhinah.

When we are one in the presence of God, we are able to generate sacred energy. In other words, we create possibilities in our lives that we would not be able to begin to believe existed were we not solidly grounded spiritually. That grounding releases the generative energy of God's glory and presence that acts as a light drawing us deeper into the other eight sefirot.

Once connected internally, the sefirot, like the Hindu *chakras*, elevate our consciousness and work together. We, as individual human beings, may need to work on certain characteristics within ourselves over a lifetime. By understanding what these characteristics are through the sefirot, we have an opportunity for knowledgeable transformation. For example, if I am not sufficiently aware of the Shekhinah, I need to develop prayer techniques in order to become attentive to the presence of God in the immanent world. The Kabbalah states: "In the flow of the holy spirit, one feels the divine life force coursing the pathways of existence, through all desires, all worlds, all thoughts, all nations, all creatures."[23] With such an emphasis on immanent presence, one would develop a certain confidence in being able to experience Shekhinah in the world and recognize that because of Shekhinah's pervasiveness, the transformation of awareness definitely has to do with my own attentiveness.

> The essence of divinity is found in every single thing—nothing but it exists. Since it causes every thing to be, no thing can live by anything else. It enlivens them, its existence exists in each existent.
> Do not attribute duality to God. Let God be solely God. If you suppose that Ein Sof emanates until a certain point, and that from that point on is outside of it, you have dualized. God forbid! Realize rather, that Ein Sof exists in each existent. Do not say, "This is a stone and not God." God forbid! Rather, all existence is God, and the stone is a thing pervaded by divinity.[24]

The Journey

If one enters the journey of the ten sefirot, one enters the mystical journey of life eternally present in the here and now within one's own being.

THE JEWISH MYSTICAL VIEW: THE KABBALAH

The Kabbalists knew well how to contact the foundational center of Being. Indeed all medieval mystics, whether Jewish, Christian, or Muslim, touched a reality beyond the normal space-time continuum of the medieval worldview. These masters saw beyond the edge of their known universe into the One God, what the Kabbalists call *'Ein Sof.* That is, they knew, through their own vision, that the visible universe, their everyday reality, was an emanation of the invisible. And what they saw was the patterning of the creation beginning not in the visible realm, but in Being itself.

Chapter 4

THE THEOLOGICAL VISIONS OF CHARTRES CATHEDRAL AND THE ABBEY CHURCH OF SAINT-DENIS

Chartres Cathedral and the Glory of God

It is difficult to put into words the experience of entering the sacred space of Chartres Cathedral. The effect of the cathedral is one of being thrust back in time to the late Middle Ages. This was an era of Christian history that expressed the glory of God through every possible medium. The architecture of the cathedral, the stained glass, the stone sculpture, the labyrinth, the music—all these elements combine to draw one into the Divine Mystery (see fig. 4).

THE SEVEN LIBERAL ARTS

Before the University of Paris became the premier center of learning in the thirteenth century, the Chartres Academy was one of the foremost scholastic institutions in medieval Europe. Here were taught the basic medieval curriculum of the seven arts, the *trivium* and the *quadrivium*. The *trivium* consisted of grammar, rhetoric, and dialectic, the *quadrivium* of arithmetic, geometry, astronomy, and music. For medieval theologians, who also studied philosophy, knowledge developed one's interior Godliness. Ignorance was associated with distance from God.

The purpose of each of the seven liberal arts was the development of the religious senses. One was educated to be a fuller human being by studying these areas of learning, which date back to Greco-Roman times. In fact, it was an African gram-

Fig. 4: Interior of Chartres Cathedral.

marian in the fifth century who personified the seven liberal arts. Martianus Capella, in a romance entitled: *The Marriage of Philology and Mercury*, described the union of the god, Mercury, with Philology. Today, we define *philology* as the study of linguistics. Philology comes from the Greek, meaning "love of words"—*philein*, to love, and *logos*, word.

THE PERSONIFICATION OF THE ARTS

On their wedding night, Mercury presents his bride with personifications of the seven liberal arts as her wedding gift. These personifications change over time. During the Middle

Ages they are transformed into unique characters that were sculpted and painted. At Chartres, the seven liberal arts are carved on the royal portal. In fact, in the twelfth century, Chartres was the refuge of the Greco-Roman tradition, "the stronghold of classical learning."[1] John of Salisbury, who fought to maintain the classical curriculum at Chartres, had this to say about the influence of the classics on Christendom: "If we see further than they, it is not in virtue of our stronger sight, but because we are lifted up by them and carried to a great height. We are dwarfs carried on the shoulders of giants."[2]

Grammar is a woman in a long mantle carrying a whip, with two children at her knees, their heads immersed in their texts.[3] *Dialectic* is a woman carrying a scorpion at the old west porch at Chartres—the reward of speaking with an acerbic tongue, no doubt. *Rhetoric* is shown with her stylus writing on tablets, an eloquent gesture symbolizing her fluency. One gesture says it all; she needs no artifice. If one knows how to use language well, and is practiced at public speaking, one reaches out to others with no other motive than to communicate well. Furthermore, that elegance can be spiritually applied to other activities. Language here would be understood as enrichment, the skill of having learned language so soundly that language becomes an art—an art form expressed through the voice and body, intonation, and gesture.

Arithmetic, Music, and *Astronomy* all have representatives, as do the other liberal arts who are either the inventors of the art—like Pythagoras in arithmetic—or a person who represents that art. Pythagoras also represents music as he was thought of as the inventor of the laws of music.

Astronomy has Ptolemy. All seven liberal arts have both a female representative and a male counterpart, who balance the representation in stone. One of my favorite representatives is Aristotle, who is dipping his pen into an inkpot at Chartres under the auspices of the already-described figure of dialectic.

"Isidore of Seville proclaimed Aristotle as the father of dialectic, and the whole Middle Ages echoed him."[4] We know that Thierry, who was a teacher at Chartres, may have been the first person to teach Aristotle's complete works, hence, Chartres may well be justified in laying claim to being the "true cradle of scholasticism."[5]

THE LABYRINTH

The representatives of the humanities are only some of the artistic and religious treasures Chartres has to offer us. One of the foremost is its eleven-circuit labyrinth, which dates from the early thirteenth century.

For medieval people the labyrinth symbolized the pilgrimage to Jerusalem. The medieval pilgrim undertook such a journey to become closer to God or as an expression of repentance. While actual travel to the Holy Land was not an option for many people, traveling either to one or more cathedrals was well within one's grasp. Travelers by the thousands prayed the labyrinth at Chartres by walking meditatively or (for repentance) on their knees.

The labyrinth at Chartres is 42 feet in diameter and the circular length in its entirety is 861 feet (at its widest 16.4 meters from pillar to pillar).[6] It is divided into four quadrants, and its readily visible four arms symbolize the cross of Christ. This labyrinth also contains an invisible thirteen-pointed star. The star is symbolic of contemplation, of Mary as the representational Queen of Heaven. Her star is the medieval mystical rose.

Mary's rose is our contemplative being. To walk the labyrinth is to enter into our true archetypal nature within, as a rose. The form is mandalic and natural. Flowers in different cultures are living symbols, crystalline structures that spiral, turn, and with loveliness unmatched, turn our senses toward an appreciation of the aesthetic.

MEDIEVAL AND RENAISSANCE SPIRITUALITY

The spiral circle of the labyrinth mandala is the curvaceousness of the rose and the human representation of the rose geometrically. The word *mandala*, which is used in many Eastern religious traditions, comes from Sanskrit and symbolizes the cosmos. The universality of mandalic forms is one of the great visual and spiritual bridges between cultures. Examples abound around the world. For example, the Tibetan sand mandalas are labyrinths to steady the mind and empty preconceptions, whereas the Hopi labyrinth, like the Christian representations, symbolizes transformation and new life.

To the Christian the labyrinth is a metaphor for life's journey and for the inward spiritual journey. Even today its value as a spiritual tool is being rediscovered, and many churches, retreat centers, and schools are establishing labyrinths. At Grace Cathedral in San Francisco, a replica of the Chartres labyrinth is now a pilgrimage site for modern seekers on the West coast.

VISUAL LEARNING AIDS, MEDIEVAL STYLE

In an era when the average person could not read, the art in medieval Christian churches served to teach the people about their faith. Whether through intricate, dazzling stained-glass windows, stately statues, or sumptuous carvings on doors and portals, medieval churches are populated with figures from the Old and New Testaments as well as from later Christian history—the Communion of Saints in glass, marble, and wood. The Christian could walk prayerfully through the church, "meet" these important figures in her or his faith history, and meditate upon biblical scenes depicted in the church art. Chartres Cathedral is no exception.

On the north portal we see statues of important persons from the Old and New Testaments who prophesied or prefigured Christ. There's Isaiah, for example, who foretold that a "shoot shall come out from the stump of Jesse, and a branch shall grow out of his roots" (Isaiah 11:1, NRSV). Jeremiah, a figure or "type" of Christ's Passion, holds a Greek cross. John the Baptist, wearing his camel hair tunic and points to a medallion of the Lamb of God. And Simeon holds the baby Jesus in his arms in a scene from the presentation in the temple. Among the Old Testament stories depicted is the narrative of creation showing Adam emerging from behind the head of God. Both the south portal and the west portal (also known as the royal portal because of its elegant statues of kings and queens from the Old Testament) contain scenes of the last judgment, a highly popular theme in the Middle Ages. On the west portal Christ, surrounded by the symbols of the four evangelists, holds the Book of Life in his left hand and raises his right hand as if in blessing. In this image of Christ, the artist appears to have tried to depict both his divine and his human natures; it is unique in medieval cathedral sculpture. Also on the west portal, we find a series that may offer evidence of a local cult revering Mary as healer of mothers and infants: it depicts the story of Mary's parents, Sts. Anne and Joachim, who struggled with infertility before Mary's birth.

In the interior of the cathedral, the stained-glass windows—there are between 150 and 170 of them—are like glowing jewels through which shine more scenes from scripture and popular piety. They include the last judgment, the passion, and resurrection, Old Testament kings and prophets, the four evangelists, and the elders of the apocalypse. The anonymous medieval artists and craftsmen who set out to glorify God and to educate and edify the people have left us marvelous clues to the spirituality of medieval Christianity as well as countless treasures through which the modern-day visitor, too, can reach God.

The Abbey Church of Saint-Denis:
A Heaven of Stained Glass

The Gothic tradition of stained-glass windows as panorama of contemplative light begins with Abbot Suger. Abbot Suger was the spiritual head of the Abbey of Saint-Denis from 1122 to 1151 and advised several French kings, among whom was his long-standing friend Louis VI. The church on this site had been the burial place of the French kings since the time of Clovis, the first king of the united Frankish nation. King Dagobert I (ruled 628–637) founded the abbey and, in the following centuries, the church underwent several renovations.

THE TWELFTH-CENTURY RENOVATION

The abbey owes its present magnificence largely to King Louis VI (1081–1137). This was the era of great church construction, a time when humans glorified God through these splendid architectural monuments, and Louis VI wanted the abbey to become the spiritual center of France. Under his patronage and encouragement, Abbot Suger, between 1135 and 1137, set about renovating Saint-Denis so that it would reverently celebrate the glory of God and honor both St. Denis, one of the patron saints of France, and the representative of God on earth, namely the king himself. A famous parallel in Germany is the great Cathedral of Cologne, whose Prince-Archbishop, Reinald von Dassel (reigned 1156–1167), brought the purported bones of the three Magi to his cathedral in order to attract large numbers of visitors. To this day people flock to this, the foremost church in the Rhineland, to see the beautiful Shrine of the Three Kings.

Because of his thorough remodeling of the abbey church, Abbot Suger is credited with beginning Gothic art and architecture in France. He himself seems to have participated actively in the remodeling work. The great art historian Erwin Panofsky records how Suger went in search of some beams and wrote, "Quickly disposing of other duties and hurrying up in the early morning, we hastened with our carpenters, and with measurements of the beams...."[7] Suger was influenced by the fifth-century theological writings of Dionysius the Pseudo-Areopagite, who described the universe as consisting of the "Father of Lights" (God), the "first radiance" (Christ), and the "smaller lights" (the people). In rebuilding the church, Suger desired to get closer to this "one true light," a goal he achieved through his use of heightened architecture as well as by his passion for light in the church.

Like Chartres, Saint-Denis has its depiction of the last judgment, one of the most popular themes in Gothic cathedrals and churches. It shows Christ on his throne, surrounded by Mary and the twelve apostles, while below them the dead are rising from their coffins. (It is no coincidence that the famed sequence *Dies irae, dies illa* dates from this era.) The twenty-four elders of the apocalypse also appear. Perhaps the most renowned aspect of Gothic architecture initiated by Suger at Saint-Denis is the rose window. In 1258 the Cathedral of Notre Dame in Paris replicated the design of the beautiful rose window of Saint-Denis. Characteristic of Saint-Denis as the burial place of monarchs is the "royal" theme prominent in some of the artwork: some museums in France have preserved examples from earlier renditions of the abbey church, notably depictions of Old Testament kings that allude to the divine right of the French kings.

Suger fulfilled his ambition to make the Abbey of Saint-Denis a "monument of applied theology."[8] He wanted it to express the incarnation of God in matter, revealed through the beauty of light and color. Jesus embodies the divine, and the stained glass narratives tell us his parables. Yet, the building's structure is in itself a theology of Christian belief. Suger, in his own words, shares with us so many centuries later his rationale for creating the beauty of stained glass, for collecting the most precious of jewels, and for ornamenting the house of God, first quoting from the Hebrew Scriptures:

> Every precious stone was thy covering, the sardius, the topaz, and the jasper, the chrysolite, and the onyx, and the beryl, the sapphire, and the carbuncle, and the emerald. To those who know the properties of precious stones it becomes evident, to their utter astonishment, that none is absent from the number of these (with the only exception of the carbuncle), but that they abound copiously. Thus, when—out of my delight in the beauty of the house of God—the loveliness of the many-colored gems has called me away from external cares, and worthy meditation has induced me to reflect, transferring that which is material to that which is immaterial, on the diversity of the virtues: then it seems to me that I see myself dwelling, as it were, in some strange region of the universe....[9]

For the abbot, all the muck of the Middle Ages disappears through the riches of stained glass and precious jewels. He enters another region of the universe beyond pain and suffering.

A COMMUNAL ENDEAVOR

Although people had mixed reactions to the wealth demanded by cathedral building, enough work was generated so that an entire village might be employed for over a hundred years and would proudly display their handiwork, a continuing source of inspiration and commerce, when people on pilgrimage stopped to worship and buy goods in the town. Medieval towns had a fine combination of services mingling genuine spirituality and human material survival. Today, we would call this community self-sufficient. This is why we often see, at the tops of cathedral pillars, not angels, but the people and animals that helped build the cathedral. Modern pilgrims are puzzled when they see peasants and oxen drawing the carts that carried the quarried stone as the top of the hierarchical ladder on the stone pillars; but for medieval souls, animals, nature, and all the workers built the cathedral together.[10] In fact, it may have been the only community event that joined all classes in a mutual endeavor of beauty and work for their shared prayerful worship.

Medieval people loved their cathedrals and basilicas. To those whose lives were filled with hunger, disease, high infant mortality, war, and the constant evidence of the world as a "vale of tears," these great churches stood as another reality that was not numbed with pain. For Suger and the builders of Chartres, the cathedrals and other great churches were truly not just an escape from life's miseries, but an entrance to and taste of paradise on earth.

Chapter 5

"AND WE WALKED OUT ONCE MORE BENEATH THE STARS": DANTE

The Giotto Dante[1] is one of the only known portraits of the poet by someone who actually knew him during his lifetime. Giotto painted the portrait, displayed now in the Bargello in Florence, probably after Dante's death. I always find the portrait surprising in its anticlimactic quality. One expects a spectacular portrait of such a literary giant, a portrait at the very least expressing in line and gaze the terrible tragedies Dante endured, of betrayal and exile from his beloved city, Florence. An inspired portrait perhaps, with Beatrice guiding her Dante into the medieval mystical rose of paradise.

Giotto's actual portrait, however, is somber (see fig. 5). Dante is portrayed quietly, without Giotto's usual emotion, with an almost iconic, inward-looking expression, that of a human being who gazes, reflects, and internalizes what he sees. This poet is a contemplative—ageless, without deceit.[2] Recall that T. S. Eliot declared, "Dante and Shakespeare divide the world between them—there is no third."

Dante Alighieri (ca. 1265–1321) "walked out once more beneath the stars" because he had been through the inner circles of hell. And although he was a true medieval for whom hell was

Fig. 5: Giotto di Bondone (1266–1336), detail of
The Last Judgment with portrait of Dante.

a terrifyingly real domain, the hell he describes is something we too can relate to because it is a place of timeless metaphor.

Innumerable medieval depictions exist of hell and the Last Judgment, but most cannot approach the multiple layers of subtle mythological, literary, psychological, and spiritual meaning that Dante describes in *The Inferno*. Certainly others have devils and the Devil, the tortures of hell; but to our modern ears, these seem like the platitudes of a literal imagination. Dante's *Inferno* is internal as well; it is a place within, without positive change or possibilities. It is a place of lost hopes. And the worst loss is being unable to be in and enjoy the presence of God.

The *Commedia*, a trilogy composed of the *Inferno*, *Purgatory*, and *Paradise*, mirrors the classical mystical stages of purgation, illumination, and union with God. The *Commedia* "is a glorification of the ways of God, but it is also a sharp and great-minded protest at the ways in which men have thwarted the divine plan."[3]

Dante's *Commedia* is the epitome of medieval thought, and he is the last synthesizer of medievalism before the humanism of the Italian Renaissance. For Dante as a true medieval citizen, the goal of human life, the *summum bonum*, is union with God. Whether in great cathedral architecture, theology, or the frescoes of Giotto, the alpha and omega of life is to experience the divine presence. Thus, Dante models the *Commedia* on the classic mystical stages of purgation, illumination, and union with God.

Purgatorio

Purgatory has a dual meaning for Dante, the literal and the allegorical. The concept of purgatory as an actual place has no obvious biblical foundation; yet, in medieval times, entire theologies and works of art were created depicting purgatory. Purgatory differs from hell in that it offers an intimation of hope, something impossible in hell. Purgatory is the place where *you* work on your salvation, and ultimately enter into heavenly paradise.

In contrast to purgatory, in Dante's hell there is absolutely no redemption. Each circle of hell draws us downward, by gravity as it were, so that the hierarchy of evil is reversed. That is, the worst sins are portrayed in the lower circles at the bottom. Dante locates the lesser sins at the top entrance to hell and depicts them with comparatively mild imagery. The most severe punishments are grotesque even to us moderns inured to the popular media. For example, the hell of Count Ugolino de' Gherardeschi is eternally to sink his teeth "like a mastiff's 'gainst the bone, / firm and unyielding"[4] into Archbishop Ruggieri's skull. That is their hell, literally bound together in this same repulsive act, for all eternity. Ugolino and his children had actually been starved to death in the tower at Pisa by order of Archbishop Ruggieri. Dante relates the heart-wrenching story of the children offering themselves to be eaten by their own father, Ugolino. Ugolino refuses, and lives to see his children slowly die of starvation, whereupon he, too, breathes his last.

Dante has us sympathize with Ugolino even though Ugolino is possessed by revenge and hatred after his death. We can understand the parental despair of Ugolino, which leads him, even in hell, to be unable to let go of his own cruel obsession for vengeance.

Allegory

Medieval people thought allegorically. Like our medieval ancestors, we hunger for story, allegory, mythos, but often we succumb to the literalism of our empirically-oriented culture. The Middle Ages were all allegory, whether through biblical stories contained in the medium of stained glass, or the tales of chivalry, or the songs of the troubadours.[5] Spiritual and moral meaning, for example, was expressed through biblical stories, social meaning through the tales of chivalry, and emotional relationships through the songs of the troubadours. Our own contemporary culture, in contrast, does not really offer much of right-brain metaphorical, intuitive reflection on the basic existential questions of life's meaning and purpose.

In the *Commedia*, Dante writes allegorically and literally simultaneously. He gives us facts, people, places, and events. In fact, historians have learned much about medieval Florence through Dante's writings. The universal poet and wise spiritual sage is, however, the allegorical Dante: "From the most sacred waters I returned remade in the way that trees are new, made new again, when their leaves are new...."[6] This is the guide of the spiritual journey, the character Dante in the *Commedia*, about to leave purgatory and enter paradise.

Dante is original in that he is both the author of the *Commedia* and makes himself the character, Dante, who leads us through the stages of the journey: Purification, Illumination, and Union. Jorge Luis Borges commented; "We believe Dante so profoundly…because the Commedia is written in the first person."[7]

Pilgrimage and Love

Dante's quest is a search for the Beatific Vision. His medieval pilgrim not only goes on a pilgrimage of the soul, but also awakens to the guidance of love, symbolized by Dante's beloved Beatrice.

People today are sometimes cynical concerning Dante's single-minded love for Beatrice. It is true that a girl named Bice did exist.[8] Dante glimpsed her from afar as a boy of nine and fell in love with her. She married someone else and died in 1290, when Dante was still a young man of twenty-five. He nearly went insane when Beatrice died. It is only because of an epiphany, of which he writes in the *Paradiso* XXXI: 69, that he overcomes his grief, having now seen the woman he will call Beatrice in paradise.

Beatrice symbolized the powerful transformative gift of love; so much so that Dante's daughter took the name "Sister Beatrice" when she made her profession as a nun. Dante's internal guide, Beatrice, ascends the ladder of spiritual evolution and leads Dante into Eternal Bliss.

> Like a lark that soars in rapture to the sky,
> first singing, and then silent,
> by the last sweetness of its soul's own cry—

such seemed that seal of the Eternal Bliss
that stamped it there, the First Will at whose will
whatever is becomes just what it is.[9]

And, in Sinclair's translation; "Like the lark that soars in the air, first singing, then silent, content with the last sweetness that satiates it, such seemed to me that image, the imprint of the Eternal Pleasure by whose will all things come to have their being."[10]

Dante is speaking of the very essence of the Divine within us: "Whatever is becomes just what it is." Such is the seal of "Eternal Bliss." And later in Canto XXVIII Dante, referring to Beatrice, "But she, knowing what yearning burned in me, began thus—with so rapturous a smile God seemed to shine forth from her ecstasy."[11] That ecstasy is Eternal Bliss. Dante's spirituality is not simply a personal mystical experience but one in tune with the universe: "at the still point, there the dance is." "This heaven does not exist in any place but in God's mind...." This insight witnesses to the *Commedia*'s universality and timelessness, despite the historical particulars of Italian people, places, and events in the thirteenth century.

What is the Dantean mind of God? If we examine each of the lines from the verses above, we see that, in these succinct images, there exists a profound intellectual and spiritual cosmology: "The order of the universe...." The way the universe is ordered, the theoretical physical "entities" to which, after Dante's time, we give the names, *gravity*, *speed of light*, *space-time continuum*, operate within definite perimeters. Everything in our visible world and the invisible realities that hold matter together, operate within patterns that express order in the universe. As Alain of Lille famously put it more than a century before Dante: "God is an intelligible sphere whose center is everywhere, and whose circumference is nowhere."

For Dante, once we enter paradise and watch the universe working, we are able to comprehend how the universe is ordered. We *know* that reality ultimately originates at the center. For God "dwells with you" (John 14:17).

Jesus' saying, "Believe me that I am in the Father and the Father in me" (John 14:11), is the very core of Dante's universe. Dante understood the Christian mystery of death and resurrection. Speaking before he is crucified, Jesus says, "In the world you have tribulation, but be of good cheer, I have overcome the world" (John 16:33). Dante understood the power of Jesus at the center with God.

> O Light Eternal fixed in Itself alone,
> by itself alone understood, which from Itself
> loves and glows, self-knowing and self-known.[12]

To achieve the Light Eternal—the Beatific Vision—is to have experienced conversion: to have made the arduous journey from darkness to light, from death to life; it is to have embraced the cross, to have experienced Good Friday in order to attain the joy of Easter. As Dante expressed it at the culmination of his great work: "But now my desire and will, like a wheel that spins with even motion, were revolved by the love that moves the sun and the other stars."[13]

We must go through the darkness to attain the light; we must traverse hell in order to attain heaven, "the love that moves the sun and other stars." Dante challenges us to face the real and potential ugliness within. Only when we look at ourselves and see our own sinfulness and the most appalling possibilities of our decisions and actions can we continue on that journey. Although a Platonist in so many ways, Dante follows Plato's student, Aristotle, in recognizing that human beings may choose evil even if they *know* the likely consequences. Dante is not naïve. Hence, his appeal lies in the fact that we know he made hurtful choices in his own life, and later his remorse develops the wisdom so obvious in the *Commedia*.

A universal spirit such as Dante cannot, however, be limited by the wrongful choices of one life; he is much broader and profounder than that. It is because Dante understands himself that he can imaginatively enter into levels of hellish experience not his own. He can take the hurt and sin of his own life, apply that shadowy realm of psychological and unique historical circumstances, and give us a masterpiece of psychological, mythological, and spiritual profundity.

Vision of Paradise, Then Back to Hell

Faith before reason is how the *Commedia* begins; it is why the pagan poet Vergil is Dante's guide and why Vergil, although Dante's hero, cannot rise to the bliss of being in God's presence. Dante identifies so deeply with Vergil that the sympathy he feels for Vergil's predicament is palpable. Like all the great humanists and philosophers Dante admired, including Socrates, Plato, Diogenes, Seneca, Euclid, Ptolemy, Avicenna or Ibn Sina, and Averroes or Ibn Rushd, Vergil was not Christian.[14] In Dante's world they cannot be saved. These souls enjoy a natural light, but they cannot know the light of Christ.

Vergil and the other philosophers have a special place in the *Inferno*, but they know virtually nothing of the redeeming love of God. Thus, Dante treats Vergil with tremendous tenderness and empathy.

Why the *Inferno* Still Speaks to Us Today

When he lived in Florence as a young man, Dante would alternate between visiting the Franciscans at Santa Croce and the Dominicans at Santa Maria Novella. He was influenced, by the spirituality of both: on the one hand, the Franciscan emphasis on faith and nature, and on the other hand, the Dominican spirituality that is at once down-to-earth and nourished by intellectual study. Dante had studied Plato and Aristotle. He had obviously studied Vergil, and had been influenced by Homer, Lucan, Horace, and Ovid, among others. Like a master tapestry-maker, he wove the philosophies, epics, poems, and theologies into a masterful work recognizable in the *Commedia*.

Those who were Christian—such as Bonaventure and Thomas Aquinas—have the privilege of being in Dante's heaven. If they were not Christian, he gives them a privileged place in hell.[15] Hell for Dante is not so much a place of fire and brimstone as it is a place of hopelessness: "Abandon all hope ye who enter here."[16]

If we take Dante's vision as a metaphor, the personal and social perceptions of Christendom's greatest poem remain timeless. One can only have hope if there is the hope of experiencing God. If an individual chooses to sin, that choice determines the rest of their eternity. The abandonment of hope in the Dantean universe is the choice we each make to say yes or no to partnership with God in our lives.

There is no middle ground because the first people Dante meets in hell are the "nearly soulless / whose lives concluded neither blame nor praise."[17] This is part of Dante's attitude toward human behavior; namely, we are responsible for our actions, and if we don't act, we are responsible for our omissions.

Dante does not separate hell from pain. Satan is called "The Emperor of Pain." We moderns can relate to that analogy especially if we chose to suffer. How bizarre that sounds, to "choose to suffer," but for Dante people choose much of their own pain. Pain is implicit in the human condition, but we add to it when we make decisions that put us in harm's way.

Dante is both moralistic and condemnatory. There is no middle ground, no excuse, he is difficult and pushes himself in the *Commedia* whether through hell, purgatory, or heaven, while paradoxically remaining a sympathetic character as the narrator of the *Commedia.*

Satan lives in the icy wasteland of hell and if we can say anything about Dante's depiction of Satan for our time, it is that Satan helps us identify chosen pain. Dante is sharing with us the spiritual fact of being able to make a decision not to descend into the cold and shadowy realms of violence, anger, and waste.

Dante illuminates the human potential within each of us by showing us how dreadful our decisions can be, how horrific the consequences of our actions can be. He points the way out of pain, then, and into a realm of spiritual actualization. The last verse of the *Inferno* speaks of the guidance and illumination of following the spiritual journey all the way into heaven:

> By that hidden way
> My guide and I did enter, to return
> To the fair world: and heedless of repose
> We climb'd, he first, I following his steps,
> Till on our view the beautiful lights of Heaven
> Dawn'd through a circular opening in the cave:
> Thence issuing we again beheld the stars.[18]

65

Chapter 6

RELIGION AND ECOLOGY: HILDEGARD OF BINGEN

For Hildegard, "God is Music,"[1] music one can hear and express through the experience of God's presence as a living Light permeating all creation. She was one of the greatest composers of her day and her music is now readily available.[2] Hildegard's chant melodies both soothe the soul and bring a sense of harmony and balance, which are two of the major motifs of her lifetime oeuvre.

Hildegard was a Benedictine nun and abbess, theologian, composer, physician, and herbalogist.[3] She was born in 1098 CE, and died on September 17, 1179.

Born into the upper nobility of Germany the tenth child of Hildebert and Mechthild of Bermersheim in the Rhineland, Hildegard was tithed to the monastery of Disibodenberg when she was eight years old. It was common for the wealthier noble families to give their tenth child to the church as a tithe, just as they would tithe a tenth of their harvest as an offering of thanksgiving for their prosperity and as a precautionary measure to prevent possible future catastrophes from afflicting their family. Thus the young Hildegard was placed in the care of a mentor, Jutta of Sponheim. From Jutta, Hildegard received her Benedictine religious training, balancing prayer and work. She lived a structured monastic life filled with the hymns of scripture and chanting in Latin.

After Jutta died in 1136, Hildegard was elected the leader of the community. Her trusted adviser was the monk Volmar, whom Hildegard describes as her teacher. Volmar, who remained Hildegard's confidant until his death in 1173, came to realize that Hildegard's visions were authentic and from God.

Like most women of her time, Hildegard received little formal education; however, because of Volmar, she learned patristics, and from her Benedictine liturgical and scriptural studies with Jutta, she understood Latin.[4] She refers to herself as *indocta*, unschooled, but "she was a well-schooled woman who surpassed most authors in excellence."[5] Hence, she was *docta*, educated.[6]

Hildegard was encouraged by Bernard of Clairvaux, among others, who sent parts of Hildegard's *Scivias* (Know the Ways of God) to Pope Eugenius III, a Cistercian like himself.

> Final approval of her prophetic charism was given by the Cistercian Pope Eugenius III at the synod in Trier in 1147–48. Bernard of Clairvaux and the archbishop of Mainz had sent a partial copy of *Scivias* to the Pope and had intervened on her behalf. An extraordinary thing happened as a result: the Pope read aloud to the assembled bishops from this book by a woman. All the bishops applauded when Bernard urged the Pope to "not allow such a brilliant light to be covered by silence but rather to confirm this charism through his authority." The Pope consequently wrote to Hildegard, encouraging her in the name of Christ and of St. Peter to make known all that was revealed to her in the Holy Spirit; he practically ordered her to write.[7]

Bernard himself wrote to Hildegard:

> How can we teach you or exhort you when an inner instruction is already present and the gift of the Spirit instructs you about everything? Much more to the

point, we beg and desire that you always remember us before God and also those who are tied to us in spiritual community.[8]

While working on *Scivias*, the word "I" disappeared from Hildegard's writings. She "consented to become a feather on the breath of God."[9] What this meant spiritually in terms of Hildegard's inner perspective was that she had surrendered herself, her "I," to God. Constantly aware of guidance by the Holy Spirit, she did not presume to know God's will but waited for instruction.

In 1114, when she believed she was instructed by God to write her visions,[10] she "began to preach and make public her visions through written texts."[11] Hildegard scholar Barbara J. Newman describes Hildegard's obedience to God and the positive results of her decisiveness:

Measured in purely external terms her achievements are staggering. Although she did not begin to write until her forty-third year, Hildegard was the author of a massive trilogy that combines Christian doctrine and ethics with cosmology; a compendious encyclopedia of medicine and natural science; a correspondence comprising several hundred letters to people in every stratum of society; two saints' lives; several occasional writings; and, not least, a body of exquisite music that includes seventy liturgical songs and the first known morality play....

We must not underestimate the courage she needed as the first woman, to the best of her knowledge, to take up wax tablets and stylus in the name of God. Even greater, perhaps, was the daring required to embark on her career as a public preacher of monastic and clerical reform. This mission led her to undertake four prolonged preaching tours, beginning at the age of sixty; she spoke mainly to monastic communities, but on occasion addressed clergy and laity together in the public squares.[12]

The Illuminations

Hildegard's visions were drawn at her own scriptorium around 1165, most likely by her own nuns. As was standard policy at the time, art was a communal activity and individual artists often did not record their names. The original illuminations are no longer extant, but we do have a hand-copied and hand-painted facsimile on parchment, painted during the years 1927–1933, by the nuns of Eibengen from the originals. The originals were moved to Dresden for safekeeping during World War II and have since disappeared.[13]

Hildegard had been having visions since childhood. She "possessed from an early age a gift for prophecy and clairvoyance whose legitimacy was freely acknowledged by her contemporaries."[14] She describes herself in the visionary state as "awake and seeing with a pure mind and the eyes and ears of the inner self."[15]

One of Hildegard's most striking visions is of the *Trinity* (fig. 6). At the center is a sapphire-blue Christ. This Christ is human and otherworldly at the same time and might be male or female. In this instance, gender does not seem important to Hildegard. The figure's divine-human representation is paramount: What Hildegard calls the "living Light." The Trinity is a fiery eye with the figure of Christ as the pupil. Both hands have upraised palms in the "Fear not" gesture,[16] while emanating the living light of Divine Love into all of creation.

Fig. 6: Hildegard of Bingen,
The Trinity.

We have, in the Trinity, three of Hildegard's theological themes that weave through so much of her spirituality:[17] First, that God is maternal and paternal. Second, "*viriditas*, her own coinage for the greening power of the world,"[18] is the Holy Spirit energizing all of creation. And third, the emphasis on wisdom as spiritual gift.

Greening

In Hildegard's system the concept of *viriditas*, or greenness, refers to the sap, the life force that sustains natural creatures. In human beings *viriditas* is the Spirit, the lifeblood that keeps them alive. Although Hildegard did not know about photosynthesis[19] and how important trees are in keeping the air purified, her observation of the world around her gave her the intuitive understanding of a force that sustained living things.

In her *Symphonia* Hildegard hails the "Spirit [as] the source and origin of all life. The life of life."[20] All the creatures of the earth manifest the glory of God. Human beings are either alive with *viriditas* or dead with *ariditas*, dryness. Like the rest of creation, we need our own greening power, the Spirit, to live fully. Hildegard drew a parallel between the human spirit and plant life: without our being "watered" by the Spirit, we dry up. *Aridities* is a terrible fate, whether to a human being, a tree, or a plant. To die of thirst because one has no "soul water" is simply a waste in Hildegard's fertile spiritual garden. Thus Hildegard does not separate the landscape of an interior ecology from the macrocosm. The needs we have within to refresh ourselves, nourish our souls, water our spirits, and cultivate our lives with positive influences, are similar to the ecological needs of the natural world around us. Hildegard sees our contemplative purpose as coming to be closer to God and experiencing God's presence. Our ecological understanding is no different. The closer we come to God, the more we experience God's presence in the natural world.

In Hildegard's *Illuminations* Vision Four: Soul and Body contains the "analogy of a tree to the soul":

> The soul in the body is like sap in a tree, and the soul's powers are like the form of the tree. How? The intellect in the soul is like the greenery of the tree's branches and leaves, the will like its flowers, the mind like its bursting firstfruits, the reason like the perfected mature fruit, and the senses like its size and shape. And so a person's body is strengthened and sustained by the soul. Hence, O human, understand what you are in your soul....[21]

A Gift of Celebration

For Hildegard, the life we have on earth is a gift of celebrating *viriditas.* As an herbalist, Hildegard understood the ways of nature. She saw connections we empirically comprehend today through science. Hildegard's herbalism was a product of the knowledge of her time handed down to her in concert with her own observations of how nature worked.

"It has been established that Hildegard of Bingen personally attended, treated, and healed the sick."[22] She was trained in botany and the administration of medicinal herbs, and could help people maintain health through preventative measures; sometimes she healed people who were ill.[23] Often known as the first German female natural scientist and physician, Hildegard wrote prolifically on natural and medical matters. *A Study of Nature*, a work in nine books that deals with nature, plants, animals, and medicines, discusses the plant and animal worlds (including fish, birds, mammals, and reptiles), trees, the elements, stones, precious stones, and metals (or *Physica*):

> This reference book for the study of nature bears witness to Hildegard's deep love for nature and by that token to her love for God as creator. As such it can be seen as the logical and necessary complement to *Holistic Healing*, which binds theological, scientific, cosmological, anthropological, pathological, and therapeutic themes into an integrated whole.[24]

Sophia

Wisdom, *sophia*, is ours when we learn the language of *viriditas*:

> The soul is the greening life-force (*viriditas*) of the flesh, for the body grows and prospers through her, just as the earth becomes fruitful when it is moistened. The soul humidifies the body so it does not dry out, just like the rain which soaks the earth.[25]

Hildegard never separates the greening life force of the soul, enlivening the body, from wisdom. Modern commentators attribute Hildegard's holistic approach integrating body, emotions, mind, and soul to the fact that she was a woman. Her music, her medicinal herbalogy, her knowledge of anatomy, her time spent in the verdant Rhine Valley, her Benedictine balance of work and prayer, all contributed to her holism.

Wisdom, *sophia*, is one with the greening power. Our learning is made happy by the breath of wisdom, which is garnered through becoming greened.

In the West, the concept of spiritual development as a matter of becoming increasingly "greened" in wisdom is Hildegard's unique contribution. "When fulfilling the precepts of God's commandments, people, too, are the delightful and dazzling garment of wisdom. They serve as her green garment...."[26]

In Hildegard's cosmology the human being is located between God and the natural world. Humanity shares characteristics with the natural world but, because of its intellect, is close to God. This closeness to God brings with it moral responsibilities that the rest of the natural world does not have. The special *viriditas* enjoyed by humans, while parallel with that of the natural world, both challenges and inspires humans toward moral actions:

> The soul is like a wind that waves over herbs,
> is like the dew that moistens the grass,
> is like the rain-soaked air that lets things grow.
>
> In the same way you should radiate kindness
> to all who are filled with longing.
> Be a wind, helping those in need.
> Be a dew, consoling the abandoned.
> Be the rain-soaked air, giving heart to the weary.

Filling their hunger with instruction
by giving them your soul.[27]

In the words of the Benedictine Bede Griffiths: "As we…
become aware of the depth of the Spirit within, we discover this
unfathomable depth of knowledge and love opening up within
us and uniting us to one another and to the whole creation in the
light of God."[28] Griffiths plunged into the metaphysics of world
religions while resting in the center of his own Christ-centered
practice. For Hildegard, that center, which she terms the
"Heavenly Jerusalem," is a reality built here on earth through
"people touched by the Holy Spirit."[29] The Heavenly Jerusalem
is to be here now, taking care of the poor and being kind to all
creatures:

> And thus the works of the Spirit are shown to the
> faithful and holy soul just as the Heavenly Jerusalem
> is to be built spiritually…by Spirit-gifted labor. The
> greatness and loftiness of works done in the Holy
> Spirit become manifest in the measure by which the
> city is adorned with the good works performed by
> people touched by the Holy Spirit.
>
> But where did they come from, these works per-
> formed in proper justice, which adorn the Heavenly
> Jerusalem? Obviously from the heights of heaven. Just
> as the dew descends from the clouds and sprinkles
> the earth with its moisture, so do good deeds descend
> into humans and are watered by the rain of the Holy
> Spirit so that the person of faith might bring forth
> good sweet fruit and become a citizen in the heavenly
> city…the glory of God shines in the good works of
> the just so that on earth God is ever more passionately
> sought, adored, and honored.[30]

A Soul Ripe and Juicy

Hildegard wants us to realize the connection between Soul and Body. If we don't keep the soul nourished, ready for picking the ripe fruits through the difficulties of earthly life, we respond like a dead tree and cannot call on the rich, dense, juices within. "O Human, understand what you are in your soul...."

Hildegard is practical. She is a visionary who runs monasteries, gives herbs to sick people, and has been through many a cold and damp German winter. She knows very well that idealized visions of a heavenly soul without the connection to prayerful inspiration help little when the flu hits or her nuns need solid warm food. In this sense, Hildegard is much like Teresa of Avila. They are both prayerful people and theologians who are also in charge of practical matters. People depend on them. They can't afford the luxury of an ivory-tower prayer life that does not integrate spiritual experience with the world they care for. Teresa and Hildegard knew that for the people in their charge and in their own personal prayer lives, nothing replaces the time and wisdom resulting from the soul communally and personally being nourished by God. That is our sap and creates *sapientia*, wisdom.

In this verse from *Symphonia*, we are taught by the "breath of Sophia,"[31] wisdom and delight in life:

Out of you clouds
come streaming, winds
take wing from you, dashing
rain against stone;
and ever-fresh springs
well from you, washing
the evergreen globe.[32]

Today, we can comprehend why Hildegard is so important to our world. Imagine if we as a global culture understood as Hildegard did, that God is in clouds and rain. We would not pollute, we would not deny legislation to have more and more wilderness to keep our earth healthy and have people able to experience God in the mountains, forests, and by the sea.

> O teacher of those who know,
> a joy to the wise
> is the breath of Sophia.[33]

The ones who know enter into Sophia, wisdom. We never complete our learning, but are taught in the ever-new wisdom ways of *viriditas*, the greening power of God through the changes in nature.

Spring brings a certain kind of teaching and wisdom, if we are receptive. Summer basks in an increasing development of insight; fall demonstrates the bridge between God in the Transcendent, Eternal realm, and our experiences here on earth. And, finally, in the winter of life, we come closer to letting go of the body, and entering the realm of the invisible Spirit.

The Tree of Life is an analogy of our Soul and Body, and a metaphor of the macrocosmic tree of the universe. The cosmos is alive with the sap of God's living light and the laws that teach us how the transcendent is manifested in the immanent energy and matter around us.

For Hildegard, the closer her relationship to God and the more she recognized God's presence in her life, the more ecologically conscious she became. The two worked together. "As creatures and the handiwork of God (*opus Dei*), [we] are commissioned to continue God's creative work."[34] God's creative work would be a contradiction if it destroyed itself. Religious and philosophical works are being written and printed with increasing speed in our own time, to help the human community recognize the ecologically sacred.

Like Hildegard, we celebrate the sacred in people. We celebrate human spirituality and rationality, medicine and culture. We celebrate being able to sing and break bread together. We celebrate the divine in how our dog looks at us with unconditional loyalty and how hummingbirds diaphanously reflect sunlight. We celebrate the future and create for our children the return of a healthy planet as their legitimate inheritance.

Chapter 7

ISLAMIC LOVE MYSTICISM: RABI'A AND RUMI

Rabi'a Al–Adawiyya's Devotion to God[1]

It took Ibrahim Ibn Adham fourteen years to reach the Kaaba in pilgrimage, because he said long prayers at every shrine along the way...but when he got there, there was no Kaaba to be seen. "What is this?" he asked himself. "Have I gone blind?"

"No," a Voice said, "you can't see the Kaaba because it has gone out to meet a woman." Burning with jealousy, Ibrahim ran toward the outskirts of Mecca till he ran into Rabi'a, who was just arriving. He turned around, and saw the Kaaba back in its usual place. Then he turned to Rabi'a.

"What's this craziness you've brought into the world, woman?" he demanded.

"It's not I who am the author of craziness," she replied, "but you. You were crazy enough to take fourteen years to get to the Kaaba with your ritual prayer, while I, with my inner prayer, am here already."[2]

Rabi'a al-Adawiyya was born in 717 CE in Mesopotamia, modern-day Iraq. Most of the stories about and by Rabi'a cannot be accurately traced historically; they are hagiographical and brimming

Fig. 7: *Arabian Circle Pattern.*

with a mystique of holiness, giving to Rabi'a an archetypal quality universalizing her personal life and teachings.

In the above teaching of Rabi'a, the point is that consciousness of God must work from the inside out. Being a true mystic and Sufi, Rabi'a had little respect for asceticism for its own sake, and examples of her acerbic remarks to the other sages of that era, such as Ibrahim Ibn Adham, can be attributed to lessons on the difference between Rabi'a's devotional love and the outward practices of fasting, vigils, and saying "long prayers at every shrine" on the way to the Kaaba that characterize superficial piety. Rabi'a's zeal is not unique in the history of religions. One has only to look at the life of Buddha or Jesus, both of whom condemn external asceticism—cleaning the outer cup, but leaving the inside of the cup dirty.

It is fascinating, however, to look at just how much of an ascetic Rabi'a was for all her condemnations of this path. She proved in her person the difference between the asceticism that is a path in itself resulting in pride and separation from other beings, and that true asceticism, which purifies the heart, bringing one closer to God through viewing the reflection of the sacred in the world within and without.

"True devotion is for God: not to desire heaven nor fear hell."[3] Rabi'a believed that even in the spiritual life, there existed a temptation to turn away from the Beloved, either through desires that cause unhealthy attachments or through fears that block the trust necessary in any genuine love relationship. Rabi'a, therefore, is known throughout the Muslim world as the model of the selfless lover who ceaselessly seeks God first, and thereby avoids any of temptation's pitfalls. To this day, it is a compliment to be called "another Rabi'a," she who lived only for God, the second Mary.[4]

Rabi'a is the herald of love mysticism, her prayer consisting of the words: "Thou art enough for me."[5] She attained a unified God-consciousness in her life, exemplifying pragmatic holiness "at-one" with God. She was always available to people who sought for themselves a relationship of union with God. And she remained open to God's immanence in the created universe. No animal ran from Rabi'a, and when she would pray in the mountains, "all the animals, the deer and the wild asses, the goats and gazelles, came up to her, and gazed at her, and danced around her."[6]

PURIFICATION

Although the goal of the mystical journey is union with God, purification is the most important level. Without purification, God is an abstraction hidden by the veils of the false ego blocking the pathway into divine perception and reality. Rabi'a chose purification as a path of continual self-examination, especially in the higher states of mystical union when deception appears in the guise of supernatural powers or insights. This is not to say that the human being's natural state does not contain elements of enlightenment and gifts. The Sufis, in particular, believe that individuals who pass through purification will indeed exhibit such secondary characteristics. Nonetheless, as the ancient Hindu teachings also describe, the Sufis believe that these powers are not the goal of spiritual progress, nor the end of the journey.

God alone is the goal, and the powers that come with the opening of the layers of the subconscious are necessary to experience God's immanence active in a clear mind and the cycles of nature. Supernatural powers must not be used as magical toys to lure either the superficial follower, however, or the gullible disciple. The following is one of Rabi'a's teachings:

> One day Hasan of Basra saw Rabi'a down by the riverside. He came up to her, spread his prayer-rug on the surface of the water, and said: "Come sit with me and pray."
> "Do you really have to sell yourself in the market of this world to the consumers of the next?" said Rabi'a. Then she unrolled her own prayer-rug in thin air, and sat on it: "What you did any fish can do, Hasan, and what I did any fly can do. Our real work is far beyond the work of fish and flies."[7]

What is the real work Rabi'a demonstrates through her living parable? Is it not the continual purification of the psyche in order to create a space for God? Rabi'a never relinquished her belief in God's grace, and in the response an individual had to such a call.

The purgative road is a response to a deep call to oneness, a yearning that will even be capable through simplicity and honesty, to stand before one's ego and past, as partners on the God-quest embracing transparency and love.

Rabi'a believed in developing the utmost clarity of mind in order to stabilize one's psyche at the center of divine Reality. She did this internally for the most part, but practiced asceticism when necessary to achieve the emptiness that draws one into God's fullness. Rabi'a's definition of purgation is a sophisticated one. Here is where Rabi'a's intuitions become those of Sufis, for she makes statements that ontologically identify with God, with the internal self, and with the "signs of the earth," as one unified continuum.

Tawhid is faith in the unity of all, in the stage of clarifying discernment. *Tawhid* is the ability to differentiate and identify the thread of the sacred acting within one's psyche and external situations, as part of the necessary preparation for understanding, and further development into, a more complete union with Allah.

Discernment then, is a gradual enlightenment brought about through grace and effort. It is an unlearning and relearning in a new way through the guidance of God and divine principles of insight, a reconditioning process as a result of the breakdown of the false ego in the painful cleansing experienced during purification. Gradually, the mystic will honestly declare, "Thy will be done…," knowing that that will is wiser, more compassionate, and altruistic.

UNION

Rabi'a was the first Sufi to dwell extensively and thoroughly on a theology of love. The kind of union Rabi'a experienced and described has since her day been developed by some of Islam's greatest theologians, thinkers, and saints. Rabi'a called God "Friend," but more intimately, "Beloved." "Rabi'a's love of God was absolute; there was no room left for any other thought or love."[8]

She achieved a type of continuous awareness of God's presence within and without, which today we would describe as liberated awareness. In everything she touched, every person to whom she spoke, every job she performed, even every meal she cooked, Rabi'a was united to her Beloved. Her words, "my Beloved is always within my own presence,"[9] could sound quite strange, if not for the fact that Rabi'a spoke from an awakened consciousness, experiencing no separation between lover and Beloved.

One of the most famous parables of Rabi'a gives evidence of her union with God and the instruction that arose out of such oneness:

> I carry a torch in one hand
> And a bucket of water in the other:
> With these things I am going to set fire to Heaven
>   And put out the flames of Hell
> So that voyagers to God can rip the veils
> And see the real goal.[10]

For Rabi'a, nothing must stand in the way of union with God, not even fear of retribution in hell for wrongdoing, nor reward in heaven for being a good person.

Rabi'a emphasizes her unwavering position in another verse that describes the same distractions from union with God: "If you're afraid that people might discover your sins. Better start worrying they might find out about your good deeds!"[11] Ironically, here Rabi'a makes the startling statement that one's good deeds can be a greater obstacle to union with God than one's sins!

Rabi'a recognized the temptation of parading one's goodness in front of people, instead of doing what one could in mercy, yet always remaining free of praise or blame. Her insight that praise may be more of a blockage than blame is also one of the major themes elaborated on in the Hindu Bhagavad Gita. The Gita says that one must work without thought of the reward, working for God alone.

TEACHING METHODOLOGY

Rabi'a was certainly not a pedant who preached to others as a way of intellectual escapism from the essential reality of truth. Her teaching relied solely on an ontological foundation, centered in her own union with God, awareness of God's presence, and thus teaching was an outflow of a tremendous qualitative gift within. Teaching was a sharing of self, of wisdom, of divine presence.

Because Rabi'a was not interested in power or impressing with quantitative knowledge, her ideas go right to the heart of the listener, creating within the hearer a germinating garden of spiritual possibilities. Her eighth-century teaching method is accurately reflected in Goldberger and Tarule's book *Women's Ways of Knowing*:

> *Item*: Midwife-teachers assist others in giving birth to their own ideas, in drawing them out, in making the others' own tacit knowledge explicit and elaborating it.

> *Item*: Midwife-teachers do not administer anesthesia. They support the persons' thinking but they do not do the thinking for them or expect the persons to think as they do.

> *Item*: Midwife-teachers' first concern is to preserve the others' fragile newborn thoughts, to see that they are born with their truth intact, that they do not turn into acceptable lies.

> *Item*: Midwife-teachers, focus not on their own knowledge but on the others' knowledge. To them, the baby is not theirs, but the other persons'.[12]

Rabi'a's teaching called forth from the student the inner core of the self concealed behind the layers of unconscious projections and illusions. Her gift was her ability to crack through even spiritual stereotyping and help the student to birth her or his own discerning spirituality. Rabi'a's only concern was that the student reach God on her own. If the student needed help, Rabi'a was present to probe, guide, cajole, and through her own archetypal spirituality, give the student a continuous example of liberated holiness.

> "Come to the edge."
> It's too high.
> "Come to the edge."
> We might fall.
> COME TO THE EDGE.
> And they came.
> And she pushed them.
> And they flew.[13]

Rabi'a's kind of teaching was incisive, daring, and transformative. She pushed her students over the edge into their own released perceptions, creating a new understanding of who they were as human beings in relationship to their own deepest self and humanity. Perhaps one of Rabi'a's greatest gifts was the crystalline expression she conveyed of truths that normally are hidden. She never acted coy or smug, but like any great master, expertly revealed her teaching through qualitative presence, superb accuracy, and the subtle art of illustrative parables.

ECOLOGICAL IMPLICATIONS OF SAINTHOOD

Like numerous saints in different religious traditions, Rabi'a recognized the organic unity between the transcendent and immanent realms. The God who is invisibly present and transcendent is also the God who is visibly immanent and present. All sacredness, whether invisible or visible, is a tribute to Allah, to the glory of the Creator manifested through the abundance of creation.

Rabi'a longed to teach of the evident bond between Creator and creation, for she had experienced the essential relationship between transcendence and immanence in her own prayer life and reflections. She gives us a modern ecological theology because of her internal attitude to the creation nourished through her daily encounters with Allah of the near, Allah of unknowability:

> O God,
> Whenever I listen to the voice of anything You have
>   made.
> The rustling of the trees
> The trickling of water
> The cries of birds
> The flickering of shadow
> The roar of the wind
> The song of the thunder,
>   I hear it saying:
> God is One!
> Nothing can be compared with God![14]

Rabi'a's understanding of the voice of Being speaking in her own spirit, in the trickling of water, the cries of birds, and the song of thunder, points to the total embodiment of her faith and indicates why her spirituality is important to contemporary ecology.[15] She saw the material universe through a deified vision, a vision that mostly has been lost over much of the globe today.

Therefore, a religious vision such as Rabi'a's, incorporating an ontological transformation of values, is critical to the recovery of the sacred in relationship to one's own spirituality and justice issues, including the right of planetary life to exist without the infringement and desecration of violent exploitation.

Rabi'a truly lived a dedicated spirituality of reverence for all life: "This saint was credited with complete abstinence from animal products so that animals no longer fled from her."[16] Rabi'a saw every dimension of life as deserving of her reverence and respect. The ecological implications of Rabi'a's holiness are that she sought and found the thread of the sacred in all levels of being, and made no creature unworthy of her appreciative love. Allah was revealed in the small and the large, no amount of profit or so-called "progress," justified desecrating holy ground. Rabi'a's unique insight and contribution, was that she found that holy ground, everywhere.

Jalal al-Din Rumi

Rumi is arguably the best-selling poet in America.[17] All one needs to do is read a few of his poems and immediately the depth and profound spiritual insight of Rumi become apparent. Why Americans are so enamored with Rumi is no mystery. We sense in Rumi his cosmopolitan soul and instantly relate through the centuries to a person who understood pluralism from the inside out.

Rumi was born in Afghanistan in 1207 CE. His family fled the Mongol invasions and moved around 1219 to Konya, Turkey, after making the pilgrimage to Mecca. Rumi's father, Baha Walad, was a well-known intellectual Sufi, jurist, and author. Rumi grew up in a household that encouraged education, spirituality, and the understanding of the legal and historical theological development of Islam. At twenty-four Rumi took over his father's position and became "one of the most respected doctors of the Law, while he continued his spiritual practices as a Sufi adept."[18]

SPIRITUAL FRIENDSHIP AND CREATIVITY

At thirty-seven, Rumi met Shams al-Din of Tabriz, with whom he shared one of the most productive religious friendships ever recorded. Shams was the catalyst that opened the floodgates to Rumi's spiritual expressiveness through poetry: "Shams-i Tabrizi, you are at once sea and pearl, for your being entirely is naught but the secret of the Creator."[19] Shams was a wandering Sufi and embodied the freedom Rumi was ready for emotionally and poetically. "Love came into the mosque and said: 'Oh great teacher! Rend the shackles of existence! Why are you tied to prayer carpets?' "[20]

We can discern in the above lines that Rumi, with all his education, was still tied to the ritualistic practices represented by the prayer carpet analogy.[21] By integrating spiritual experience with his scholarship, Rumi would become one of the greatest poets ever to inhabit the world.

It is no coincidence that the ecstasy Rumi discovered after his transformation also led to the creation of the Mevlevi order of the whirling dervishes. That both the Sunni and Shia factions of Islam have branches of the Mevlevi order, often with connecting schools of music, is a tribute to Rumi's ability to transcend religious differences.[22]

THE WHIRLING DERVISHES

The whirling dervish achieves a release from the ego through dance entering into the spaciousness of transcendent awareness. Circling steadily

The mystic's soul circles about annihilation, even as
    iron about a magnet,
Because annihilation is true existence in his sight, his eyes
having been washed clean of squinting and error....[23]

Annihilation, *fana*, is a central concept in Sufism. For
Rumi, annihilation sets the tone of spiritual practice and achieve-
ment. Our goal is to become one with the divine presence and
the only way to do that is to annihilate the ego. "Silence! For if I
were to utter [God's] subtleties you would come forth from yourself, neither door nor roof would remain to you."[24]

Rumi's theme of "getting away from yourself" is pervasive.
He sometimes signed his poems with "the soubriquet Khamush,
the Silent, a reference to the ineffable nature of the mysteries."[25]
Getting away from yourself and being silent are joined together
in spiritual practice.

We can only hear the voice of God if we quiet the ego.
Rumi speaks of the ego as almost another person, a conditioned
entity that gets in the way of the God-experience:

When the spirit became lost in contemplation, it said this:
"None but God has contemplated the beauty of God."
This eye and that lamp are two lights, each individual;
When they came together, no one distinguished them.[26]

Rumi, poet *par excellence* and whirling dancer, was a contemplative at the core. The contemplative goal is to still the duality inside and outside, and enter into that divine beauty where
oneness shines through silent presence: "So long as you are
desirous know that this desire of yours is an idol; when you have
become beloved, after that there is no existence for desirous."[27]

THE BELOVED

The Beloved is all in all. Everything is the Beloved. To be desirous of one object is to deny the existence of God luminous in all reality. Rumi's famous *Creed of Love* describes the importance of oneness with Allah:

> One went to the door of the Beloved and knocked.
>
> A voice asked, "Who is there?"
> One answered, "It is I."
>
> The voice said, "There is no room for Me and Thee."
> The door was shut.
>
> After a year of solitude and deprivation, one returned
> and knocked.
>
> A voice from within asked, "Who is there?"
> One said, "It is Thee."
>
> And the door was opened.[28]

Like Rabi'a before him, Rumi wants only God. "The goal of the Sufi is to become so at one with God, that "me" is no longer even heard. This type of total commitment to God is possible through the necessary solitude and 'deprivation' of addictive habits of mind and body."[29] The other person we have projected within is the one we have produced by conditioning our thoughts, emotions, and body with unreal perceptions and scenarios. The sooner we can liberate ourselves from ourselves, the sooner we may enjoy the ecstatic company of the Beloved.

Rumi's theology is not to be confused with a dualism that separates body and spirit. Rumi unites the body with spiritual eyes. "Yet why should not the lover set his Heart upon [God] through whose grace the body has become wholly soul?"[30]

THE EARTH IS GOOD

The earth and her manifestations through the immanent forms of humanity and nature are good. When we become spiritually evolved, our consciousness manifests as *wholly soul*. In that state of awareness, as *wholly soul*, we learn to really enjoy our lives here on earth.

When we are caught in the trap of mentally formed idols, however, it is impossible to have the spiritual freedom simply to enjoy God's creation. Rumi's poetic images are awash with the pleasures of a full life:

> If you want the witnesses of heaven to show themselves, make your heart the companion of a mirror-polishing file![31]

> Make the house of your body a garden and rosary! Make the corner of your heart a Friday mosque!

> Then at every instant you will contemplate a unique witness bringing a rare almond-candy on a tray.[32]

Whether Rumi alludes to the smallest almond candy or a stellar astronomical observation, the presence of God is tangible for the attentive observant.

Rumi's Islamic theology is grounded in his intimate knowledge of the Qur'an:

> [Rumi's] view is surely facilitated by the positive, natural realism of the Qur'an. The Qur'an is cited and expounded throughout the *Masnavi* and, along with

the sayings (*hadith*) of the Prophet, is the source of much of the poet's inspiration. In the Qur'an, nature is Real in itself. It is not merely the overflowing of a greater reality. Rather, it is the place we are, in our bodies, experienced not in a time that is eternal or recurring but in the Now. Nature is also inherently good, unstained by sin and exalted even above the angels, so is nature a sign of God's Providence and Mercy, a blessing from [God] to be fully enjoyed and utilized.[33]

Rumi combines traditional Islamic scholarship with his unique spiritual gifts giving us new insights and metaphors for God's oneness present in material forms. Professor Nasr describes Rumi's sensual spirituality:

Rumi was one of those rare beings who possessed a kind of 'sensual awareness' of spiritual beauty, a person for whom things appeared as transparent forms reflecting the eternal essences. For him the very existence of beauty was the most direct proof of the existence of God. It can also be said that for the perceptive reader the beauty of Rumi's poetry itself is the most powerful proof of the reality of the world of the Spirit. Rumi bathed in beauty like an eagle soaring in the light of the sun and he left in his poetry as well as in the spiritual music and dance of the Mawlawi Order something of this beauty for posterity.[34]

Rumi writes, "Everywhere the secret of God is coming."[35] The secret Rumi speaks of is here *now*. Rumi's poetry helps us to see what is already before our eyes spiritually. What is before our eyes is "wholly soul" and magnificent when our senses are freed from the bondage of desire, narrow plans, and fear.

Rumi's name "literally means Majesty of Religion (*jalal*, majesty; *din*, religion)."[36] The secret of universal religiosity is living in a continuous awareness of God's presence. Rumi's majesty is that he can get us there by awakening us through his own contact with the divine. He then communicates in archetypal language what we already know intuitively.

Rumi's famous story, "The Elephant in the Dark House," demonstrates the power of illuminated perceptions and understanding:

> There was an elephant in a dark house, brought by some Hindus for exhibition. Many people went to see it and had to enter the dark stable to do so. Because it was dark they could not make out the form of the elephant at all and had to work with their hands to identify its being, each person using his palm to find the shape. The hand of one fell on the creature's trunk and he said, "*This is a water pipe.*" The hand of another touched the ear and found a fan. Another handled the elephant's leg and found a pillar, while another touched the back and discovered a throne. There were those who heard descriptions from these folk and made their own identifications, and there were still others who interpreted one shape as against another, all very diverse and contrary.
>
> Had there been a candle in each hand,
> The differences would have come from speech.
> The eye of self-perception is like the palm and hand,
> For this has power to touch but part, not whole…
>
> The spirit has a spirit calling it.
> Take the spirit home and let it drive
> For it will find the shape and size and know the whole.[37]

Chapter 8

THE INNER IS THE OUTER: FLORENCE

At dusk, the swallows begin their rondelles, circling through Giotto's campanile (bell tower). The tower, which has endured for eight hundred years, expresses both strength and delicacy. Giotto worked on it from 1334 until his death in 1337. When one sits on the steps looking upward, white painterly clouds move, scattering silver-peach light. Climbing the 414 steps is well worth the effort: the top affords a view of all of Florence, as if set back in time. One's vision moves horizontally across to the Duomo, the symbol of Florence. Brunelleschi's remarkable creation is still the fourth largest domed cathedral in the world today. The light turns golden over the threshold, and one sees one of thousands of carved statues of Mary, mother of Jesus, holding her God-child tenderly as the universe swirls overhead.

Raphael

The Madonna and Child paintings by Raphael Sanzio (1483–1520) were some of the first soft, tender mother and child depictions. Later artists tried to imitate and commercialize Raphael's originality, and the stereotyped Madonna and Child paintings began after his short lifetime. Younger than Leonardo and Michelangelo, Raphael absorbed their innovations.

The *Madonna of the Goldfinch* (fig. 8) at the Galleria Degli Uffizi has Jesus standing as a toddler looking into the eyes of the young John the Baptist. Renaissance artists placed John the Baptist in the most incongruous of settings, frequently pageants and festivals. John the Baptist reminded Renaissance people of their call to salvation; he was a heavenly herald above the turmoil of daily joys and travails and, for people surrounded by feuding cities, plague outbreaks, malaria, and any number of possible fatalities,

Fig. 8: Raphael (1483–1520), *Madonna and Child with Young Saint John and a Goldfinch.*

an ever-present symbol of hope. He is also the patron saint of Florence and his likeness appears on many church facades, frescoes, and statues.

It seems an odd sight to us, but in *Madonna of the Goldfinch*, John, in his usual tattered wild animal skins, happily holds the goldfinch for Christ to touch. Christ's hand moves protectively over the bird. Mary is holding a book for Christ to see, her other hand around John's back. Against the typical Leonardesque sfumato[1] landscape, Mary is serene and pensive, with a touch of sadness in her downward gaze toward the boys. What is Raphael's

---

overall intention? What mood does the *Madonna of the Goldfinch* convey?

The interplay among the figures suggests two scriptural verses. First, Galatians 5:25, "If we live by the Spirit, let us also be guided by the Spirit." Each figure is guided by the Spirit in a unique way. And is that not the way of the Spirit? Guiding us from within, helping us develop our individual, God-given gifts. Perhaps this was Raphael's spiritual intention. Mary appears as tender mother-protectress and guide. She holds the book and protects John's back. Christ, too, is nestled in the drapery of her clothing, his small foot resting securely on his mother's.

While John's expression is that of a toddler, Christ's is not. Christ's expression is the epitome of knowing sacrifice. He too is protector. He protects the bird and gazes directly at John, not turning away from his future sacrifice on the cross. Ironically, John is the cherubic toddler, happy and oblivious, living in the here and now. It is ironic because John usually is portrayed austerely, as the extreme ascetic that he was.

The second scriptural verse is James 3:17, "But the wisdom from above is first pure, then peaceable, gentle, willing to yield, full of mercy and good fruits, without a trace of partiality or hypocrisy." The entire painting is a wisdom painting. It is purity incarnate: the innocence of an infant, as depicted in John's playfulness, as well as the purity of Christ and Mary as Christian exemplars of developed wisdom: peaceful, gentle, open to the reasoning of Spirit's guidance.

Michelangelo

Renaissance times were lavish and complex. Scholars who try to pinpoint the Renaissance simply as a time of the flowering of Greco-Roman classicism married to Christian iconography oversimplify the period, at best. The Renaissance was a cauldron of philosophical perspectives and approaches to life. The Florentine Dominican reformer Savonarola represented the attitude of Christian puritanism, Michelangelo that of the conflict between an urbane Medician educational background and religious devotion. Leonardo da Vinci represented an empirical perspective, discovering the spiritual *through* studying the human body,[2] botany, laws of motion, even astronomy. And there were philosophers, educated and not, who viewed life as a commercial enterprise to be financially exploited.

The Medici family, who undertook the education of the young Michelangelo, were themselves influenced both by the Neoplatonism of the philosopher Marsilio Ficino and by Cosimo de Medici's love of all things Greek and Roman. The family's financial genius gave them both political power and the means to finance Michelangelo, Botticelli, Raphael, and so many other artists who may not have created at all without the Medicis' economic support.

The Medicis' deepest love, however, was for their own Christian heritage, which is why so many of the artworks commissioned by the family over time were based on biblical themes.

The bronze bust of Michelangelo at the Accademia Gallery, showing his piercing eyes and a nose broken during one of his violent temper flare-ups, images his character without mercy. I can picture Michelangelo walking the cobbled streets, dirty, marble-dusted, sweaty, and coming upon Leonardo in his fine clothes, his fashionable velvet hat with plume; the two are as different as night and day. Leonardo is all control, charm, and polish; Michelangelo is rushing to carve his name on the front of his first *Pietà*, the famous Vatican *Pietà*. He regrets this vain action for the rest of his life.

DAVID

Fig. 9: Michelangelo
(1475–1564), *David* (detail).

In 1908, after four hundred years in the outdoor Piazza della Signoria, Michelangelo's *David* (fig. 9), the colossus of thirteen feet and five inches, was moved inside the Accademia. Every tourist who goes to Florence must visit *David*. Michelangelo was the first artist to portray David without the head of Goliath. David has struck down the giant Philistine with his intellect and innocence, not with brute force. Michelangelo's sculpture makes David convey the power of God. Michelangelo's devotional trust in God exudes from every pore of the David. The body of stone pulsates with soul. David's nakedness, symbolic on many levels, spiritually conveys the power one has to overcome enemies internally and externally. David trusts in God's love and providence; all David has is his trust.

The nobility of the sculpture lies in David's unafraid nakedness. His thumb indents the sling, and Michelangelo's ability to give life to stone is obvious in every detail, from the thumb's indentation to David's bent small toe.

The determination of the eyes, the set mouth, the flare of the nostrils, portray a human being alert with every nerve at the ready and yet, Michelangelo has David in a meditative pose. Again, Michelangelo's spirituality was unfolding even during his twenties, when he sculpted David. David is alert yet meditative, poised for one of those battles that cause us to let go into surrendering trust and, simultaneously, to gather all of our developed forces, bringing to fruition our potentialities.

Michelangelo created the David from a block of marble that other sculptors had rejected because of its fault lines and discoloration. In his belief that the sculptor frees the figure from the marble, Michelangelo used the flaws of the marble from which David emerged. Michelangelo's artistic philosophy of trust, that is, the belief that the marble itself contained the form to be released, is a reflection of his spirituality. That same attitude that David incarnates, naked in front of Goliath, can be attributed to Michelangelo in front of a block of stone. The Spirit leads the unformed to the formed.

The right hand of *David* is proportionally larger than the rest of the body. The right hand symbolized Florence. Florentine to the core, wishing for the democratization of his city, Michelangelo's *David* reflects that other great Florentine exiled because of similar beliefs. Let me quote from one of Michelangelo's poems on Dante:

> Straight down from heaven, and in the flesh, he came;
> then, having seen where fires of justice burned,
> and the middling woes of good folk, he returned
> to look on God and reveal the eternal light.
>
> Bright star! Who made illustrious,
> in despite of wrong, the nest
> where I was born and bred.
>
> Dante I'm speaking of…
> that's the man I'd like to be!
>
> All there's to say of him, no way of saying;
> our eyes are blurred, his radiance too strong. [3]

FREEING THE BODY

Michelangelo freed the expressiveness of the human body. Both Michelangelo's women and men have athletic, strong bodies. In the painting *The Holy Family with Young Saint John*, Mary has strong, muscular arms and a large, sculpted body, unusual for a female representation at the time.

Italians use the word *terribilità* (dreadfulness) to describe Michelangelo's work, meaning the living presence that strikes the viewer in its presence. *Terribilità* often has poignancy almost too much to bear, much like the emotions Michelangelo describes in his poems. He had so much integrity that, rather than numb his emotions and conflicts, he channels them into his art and lives with them like restless reminders of an unsolvable puzzle.

THE MEDICI

Michelangelo's relationship with the Medici family was an unusual one. Here is how Franco Cesati tells it:

The story goes that Lorenzo noticed Michelangelo for the first time while the youngster was intent on copying the head of an aged faun, and was dumbstruck by his precocious skill: Michelangelo had in fact deviated from the model giving free reign to his own creative instinct, and had sculpted the faun with lips parted, revealing a perfect set of teeth. The Magnificent brought to his attention the fact that generally the teeth of the elderly are not all intact; Michelangelo, then, obligingly chipped one off in order to render the figure more lifelike. Subsequently, the future master of the Sistine Chapel was welcomed into the Medici household and treated like a son; he attended the school and

received a stipend, sat at the same table as Lorenzo and
had a room of his own in the palace. [4]

Their relationship was stormy because Michelangelo
wanted Florence to be a democratic republic. In fact, he fought
against the Medici, building battlements outside the city, when
the Medici were attacked. If you go to Lorenzo's tomb in the new
sacristy at the Medici chapel, you can actually see where
Michelangelo hid waiting for the Medici to retaliate. Rather than
retaliate, however, they gave the Maestro even more projects to
complete. Lorenzo's grandfather, Cosimo, and Lorenzo had supported the old, more democratic republic; however, the later
Medici, who commissioned Michelangelo to create the New
Sacristy, subverted their ancestors' idealism, disillusioning
Michelangelo.

Some art historians consider the New Sacristy to be
Michelangelo's finest sculpture. Lorenzo's tomb represents meditation; his brother Giuliano's represents action. Lorenzo's *pensieroso*, pensive warrior, reflects Lorenzo's commitment to the
humanities, especially Platonism and Christian theology. He was
an accomplished poet and ceaseless patron of the arts. The two
allegorical figures on either side of Lorenzo the *pensieroso* are
Dusk and *Dawn*, the two moments in the cycle of time considered by many to be the most poignant and lyrical. In·fact, when
Mark Twain visited Florence, staying across the Arno River, he
observed that even the city faded in the colors of dusk, blending
into the realm of dreams.

Michelangelo's male nude representing *Dusk* indeed softly
fades into the marble. Chisel marks of incompleteness magnify
that realm of dreams and unknowing connected with the coming of night. *Dawn* on the other hand, the female nude on
Lorenzo's opposite side, seems to be fully formed, rising into the
beginning of a new day in time.

Giuliano's tomb, in contrast, has *Night* on one side and *Day* on the other. Although *Day* is a male, unfinished nude, he appears weary, his face looks at us from a slightly hidden position behind the powerful shoulders. This *Day* is at the pinnacle of day, the end of the day when rest is called for, a needed reprieve from daily struggles. Michelangelo's poems ring with references to God. Psalm 23:4 seems apt in this context of divine darkness and restoration:

> Even though I walk through the darkest valley,
> I fear no evil;
> for you are with me;
> your rod and your staff—
> they comfort me.

Night is not only a figure of freshness, but is portrayed as wise, with a magnificent owl under her leg. The figure of *Night*, for me, is the female equivalent of *David*. The marble is as smooth as a pebble worn down by countless waves. Michelangelo has *Night* shimmering in the light, as if the moon's brightness were its own fecundity. Since the Maestro worked hours into the night, perhaps he felt the creative wisdom that in Florence would have come with the city quieted.

Like *David*, *Night* emanates an interior radiance, a noble presence through the muscles and the head, as in a Greek pose for contemplation. One can picture Michelangelo, with the candlelight glowing on the skin of *Night*, reaching for transcendence and mystical clarity, escaping the daily round of Florentine politics and emotional chaos.

Michelangelo's poetic lines on *Night* are famous because they are one of the few poetic expressions of his political opinion on the authoritarian Medici rule at the time; "it is the only poem in which the voice of one of his works of art is the speaker":[5]

To sleep, even more be made of stone: how these
are sweet, in a world of jobbery and shame.
Not see, not feel or hear: such fortune came
my way. Don't rouse me now. Talk softer, please.[6]

Brunelleschi: An Architectural Genius

THE DUOMO

The Duomo, the Cathedral of Florence, meaning *domus
Dei*, the house of God, is known primarily because of Filippo
Brunelleschi's dome. Today, Brunelleschi's dome is synonymous
with the backdrop of the city of Florence, giving the illusion of
being as high as the mountains surrounding the city. In fact,
homesick Florentines refer to *nostalgia del cupolone*, or "longing
for the dome." The visitor who keeps the Duomo in view and
notes how it dominates the prospect can easily relate to this.

Filippo Brunelleschi (1377–1446) was the first person since
the Romans built the Pantheon in 118 CE even to attempt such a
large cupola. Florentine to the core, Brunelleschi wanted the
largest and best structure to carry his name. Sir Banister Fletcher,
in his classic work *A History of Architecture*, states, "The Pantheon,
Rome was by far the most important temple…its most notable fea-
ture—its great dome, with a span of 142 feet—was unchallenged
until 1430–36, when Brunelleschi vaulted the crossing of Florence
Cathedral with a dome of slightly greater diameter."[7]

How was Brunelleschi able to achieve such a feat? There
exist several speculations; for example, Vasari claims that he and
his good friend Donatello took a trip to Rome, where they
"recorded the measurements of every good piece of work they
came across…regardless of time or expense."[8] Brunelleschi
would stop in amazement at the "grandeur of the buildings and

the perfect construction of the churches."[9] Hence he gained a background in Roman architecture and construction upon which he would literally build in Florence. Truly a Renaissance person, he believed that mathematical proportions created aesthetic beauty, but much more, elevated the spirit to the realm of elegance and peace.

Brunelleschi's new invention, of taking the Roman herringbone pattern of bricks and interlocking the bricks through two connected domes, resulted in a cupola that could not only support its own weight, but actually became stronger. Most cathedral domes, even Michelangelo's at Saint Peter's Basilica in Rome, were only possible because of Brunelleschi's inventiveness. I could imagine him inventing the crane on the site, a common sight at any major building project today.

Leon Battista Alberti, another great architect and Renaissance humanist, described Brunelleschi's Duomo as a form representing the entire universe. For Alberti, the ribs of the Duomo converge on infinity.

Brunelleschi's life was not serene when he worked on the Duomo. The incredible travails he endured are worth reading in Vasari. One challenge was the amount of time the workers took to descend the dome they were building in order to eat and drink. Viewing little progress, Brunelleschi had small kitchens installed on the scaffolding in order that work might progress.

SANTO SPIRITO

Brunelleschi's church of Santo Spirito, in a run-down area of the city, has nothing special on the façade; yet its architecture reveals a spiritual order of classical elements and quietude that truly sweeps the viewer away. Perhaps it is the utter simplicity of the Church of Santo Spirito, all grays and whites, without the lavish paintings of Vasari and Zuccari that cover the inside of the Duomo. That utter simplicity, hidden behind the deceptively bland façade, immediately stills any turmoil, bringing one to that still point within where the Spirit speaks in whispers. No chaos here, no grandiose Renaissance egos trying to outdo one another—just rhythm, order, and architectural beauty.

Vasari tells us that Brunelleschi, like Giotto, was physically "unprepossessing....'A lump of earth concealing veins of gold.'"[10] Uniting the aesthetic and spiritual,

> Filippo was endowed with outstanding personal qualities, including such a kind nature that there was never anyone more gentle or lovable. He was dispassionable in judgement, and he never allowed his own advantage or the interest of his friends to blind him to merit and worth in others.[11]

"Dispassionable in judgement"—the viewer may experience this quality through the cross-shaped proportions of the ground plan for Santo Spirito: completely in harmony, and the transepts precisely one-eighth the depth of the nave. Every element is technically exact. Colonnades, walls, windows, air and space, actually seem to build gentleness and peace, characteristics describing Brunelleschi's nature. When, for example, Brunelleschi and Donatello exhibited their scenes, along with those of Lorenzo Ghiberti, for the two bronze doors of the Baptistry, Florence's oldest church, they agreed that Ghiberti's were preferable. Demonstrating, as Vasari notes, "true qualities of friendship, talent untouched by envy, and sound judgement of their own abilities,"[12] Brunelleschi and Donatello spoke truthfully to the commission, which indeed chose Ghiberti. "What happy men they were! They helped each other and they found pleasure in praising the work of others. What happy men they were!"[13]

Giotto's Crucifix

The Christ figure on Giotto's crucifix at Santa Maria Novella is riveting. Hung now in the center aisle, almost thirty feet from the altar, this life-sized crucifixion has spiritual depth and poignancy. Christ has an eerie beauty, drawing one into the mystery of sacrifice. He is physically beautiful, even in death. No one could have painted this crucifixion without understanding Christ's wisdom and compassion. "The lord alone did lend him...."[14] Giotto created a Christ that reflects divinity; one has no doubt that that is where Giotto was in the divine story. He was not emotionally near the competitiveness even of good friends like Donatello and Brunelleschi. Giotto merged into that moment in time when Christ died, and he painted a Christ not agonized or looking realistically dead, but gives us the spiritual teaching of the crucifixion as an extraordinary gift.

Unlike most depictions of Mary at the cross, Giotto paints Christ's mother with a look of painful understanding. She is not hysterical, not overcome with emotion, but, as is Christ, in a state of vulnerable knowing. "Thy will be done, / On earth as it is in heaven."[15]

The della Robbia Legacy

"I am the light of the world," "EGOSVMLVXMVNDI" reads the scroll the infant Jesus holds, while cradled securely in his mother's arm. The figure of Mary is evenly balanced, and the aesthetic rules of proportional harmony are very much present in the *Madonna and Child* by Brunelleschi's friend, Luca della Robbia (ca. 1400–1482). This particular *Madonna and Child* (for there are many, exquisitely portrayed) is still at the Spedale degli Innocenti Museum.

THE INNER IS THE OUTER: FLORENCE

Luca della Robbia's contributions to Renaissance beauty are everywhere to be seen in Florence. His first known commission was for his *cantoria* or "singing gallery" for the Cathedral of Florence (1431–1438). To have received such a prestigious assignment indicates that he must have already enjoyed a reputation as an accomplished artist. The *cantoria* takes as its theme the words of Psalm 150, which calls upon a whole host of musical instruments and indeed "everything that lives and that breathes" to "praise the Lord." Typical of Luca della Robbia's predilection for charm, innocence, and naturalism, it depicts the graceful and lively figures of children singing, dancing, and making music to the Lord. Originally over the door of the Duomo's northern sacristy, the *cantoria* was taken down in 1688 and reassembled in the Museum of the Opera del Duomo.

Luca della Robbia later developed a method of making polychrome glazed terra-cotta especially suitable for outside use because it lent durability to the artwork. "…[F]or this method of working, as the inventor of it, he won the highest praise, and all ages to come [are] under an obligation to him."[16]

The resultant lustrous, polished surface was also eminently capable of reflecting light, something singularly appropriate for his earliest documented work: a lunette of the resurrection over the door of the northern sacristy of the cathedral (1442–45). In this lunette, the artist has all the figures in white against deep sky blue. Even in the semi-darkness of the Duomo, his *Resurrection* is all light and transcendence.

When the wardens of the cathedral viewed Luca della Robbia's *Resurrection*, they commissioned him to create Christ's ascension into heaven, also for the Duomo (1446). He wanted to add colors, which he did successfully in the *Ascension*. Among the white human figures, we now view natural colors for earth, plants, and trees.

In 1448, Luca della Robbia adopted his six nephews. Andrea learned sculpture and his uncle's glazing techniques, in a partnership that continued the della Robbia legacy past Luca's death in 1482.

The Spedale degli Innocenti or Hospital of the Innocenti, reputed to be the first orphanage in the world, combines Brunelleschi's architecture with Andrea della Robbia's ten medallions of foundlings in swaddling clothes. One can easily see the medallions from across the street, between the arches of the hospital.

The Bargello, the National Museum in Florence, was formerly the seat of power in Florence from the eighth century until 1502. Imagine standing at the spot where the bell would be rung to warn Florentines in case of war. Here two entire rooms are dedicated to the glazed terra-cottas of the della Robbias, including the work of Giovanni, third child of Andrea.[17]

Sandro Botticelli: Synthesizing Christianity and Neoplatonism

In the works of Florentine artist Sandro Botticelli (1445–1510), two important influences can be detected: on the one hand, that of his teacher Fra Filippo Lippi (1406–1469), and on the other, that of the Neoplatonic philosopher Marsilio Ficino (1433–1499). From Lippi, an erstwhile Carmelite monk, Botticelli learned artistic techniques—panel painting, fresco, linear perspective—as well as a certain gracefulness and a preference for subdued colors. By Ficino he was inspired to use his art to reconcile Christianity with ancient pagan philosophy, which was then enjoying a revival.

Ficino held that a spiritual circuit linked all life, including human life, to God, so that all revelation was one, regardless of whether it came from Plato, from classical myths, or from the Bible. Likewise, beauty, love, and beatitude were one, since they were phases of this same circuit. For Neoplatonists, then, for example, the goddess Venus could be identified with the Virgin Mary.

Thus it is not surprising that Botticelli's great mythological works *The Birth of Venus* and *Primavera*—the latter of which art historian Sister Wendy Beckett hails as an "allegory of life, beauty, and knowledge united by love"[18]—are, in a sense, interchangeable with his religious works, so that the wind gods in *Venus* resemble angels and the spring figure in *Primavera* strongly suggests depictions of the Virgin and her entourage of angels and saints.

Botticelli's *Madonna of the Magnificat* is another work that represents his synthesis of Neoplatonism and Christianity. The crown that illumines the figures in this painting is in itself radiant. The divine Sun illumines the crown literally from the heavens, as two angels gently lower the crown onto the Queen's head. "Light is everywhere the image of the divine truth and goodness."[19] Two other angels hold open the book of wisdom for Mary, who is writing with pen in hand as the child Jesus touches her sleeve and the book in a symbolic gesture filled with meaning and grace. Jesus seems to look up and beyond the painting. In his other hand, which his mother also clasps, he holds an open pomegranate. In Christianity the pomegranate symbolizes Christ's passion; in Greek mythology it represents resurrection. As in so many Botticellian works, the sun, the crown, the figures, the throne arm, and the landscape are flickered with gold subtly interwoven into the very nature of the theme. It is a diaphanous gold. Botticelli is known for his sensitivity in expressing the pensive nature of human beings. In *Madonna of the Magnificat*, that contemplation is radiant.

Chapter 9

SPIRITUALITY: LESSONS FROM THE MEDIEVAL AND RENAISSANCE MASTERS

We have been studying medieval and Renaissance spirituality. How can medieval and Renaissance spirituality help our world today? We know that during the Middle Ages and the Renaissance, people lived and breathed the religious ideas of their time.

People were spiritually literate. That statement alone emphasizes an enormous difference between those centuries and our twenty-first century. Today, few people are versed in a religious heritage that they can readily claim as their own from birth. The culture that surrounds us globally is popular consumerist culture—a philosophy and way of life dictated by advertising, television, the Internet, and film.[1]

Popular culture is profit-making mass media with minimal ethical values. For example, how teenagers identify themselves, what video games they play, how they dress, what makes them happy or sad, is not determined by their parents, schools, or communities; rather, it is determined economically in large part by manufacturers, advertisers, and marketers.

This is not the place for a sociological study of twenty-first-century values. Nonetheless, what we can say is that *for the most part*, popular culture in the twenty-first century is *not* steeped in spiritual heroes, ideas, and techniques for learning how to stay centered in the presence of God.

Whether one be Christian, Jewish, Muslim, Hindu, or Buddhist, unless one comes from a family or social structure that encourages one to learn about religious ideas having to do with the meaning of life, one usually does not know much about what is most significant in life. Questions about ultimate meaning are saved for philosophy courses. In fact, more than half the students I have had, especially in recent years, have little or no religious, let alone spiritual, background.

SPIRITUAL LITERACY

Each of us, regardless of our spiritual literacy, is capable of going on a spiritual quest to discover the religious roots of humanity. Hence, although the current situation is extremely pessimistic, each individual person has a chance to discover redemption. Since spiritual literacy is learned, we are in a unique position historically because for the first time in the evolution of humankind, we have extensive knowledge about the world's religions at our disposal.

We can study the wisdom traditions of Judaism, Christianity, and Islam. We can learn what each of these traditions has to say about the meaning of life and what comprises ultimate reality. And, we may seek a response to that most important question in our existential loneliness as human beings, namely, how does one enter into the presence of the sacred?

MAKING THE TRANSCENDENT UNDERSTANDABLE

In John's gospel, Jesus assures us that if we know him, if we accept Jesus as the "way, truth, and the life" (John 14:7), we not

---

only *know* God, we have *seen* God: The transcendent Divine is made understandable through the incarnation of Jesus.

We Christians have heard these words many times. Nevertheless, if we really comprehend the metaphysical implications of what Jesus is saying, the entire human endeavor gains meaning. Why? Because to look beneath an initial reading of Jesus' words to the profound experience of Jesus' teaching helps us come alive to "truth" and "life."

We begin living a life different from one defined by TV ads, or the latest gadget, car, or remodeled house. We enter into the truth of Jesus, identifying with the spiritual reality of the cosmos and the workings of nature, human endeavor, and human relationships. We find that we actually don't want all the *stuff* that popular culture pushes on us with such urgency.

It is enough to have a smaller house, a regularly maintained older car, or a washing machine that cleans the clothes even after ten years, and to ignore TV ads by recording a program when necessary and deleting the ads.

When we begin to understand the shallowness of popular consumerist culture and how our essential spiritual destiny is sapped by the energy it takes to keep up with all the materialistic demands, we stop seeking what we cannot find in acquisitiveness, and, instead, embark on studies into authentic living.

THE LANGUAGE OF WISDOM

The language of wisdom is different from religious dogmas and creeds. Wisdom requires interiority, reflection on the meaning of what we have experienced in the light of our own values.

Dogmas and creeds may enrich or detract from wisdom, depending on the individual who adheres to them. If a dogma is rigidly held without question and the individual cannot go any deeper into their own experience, the dogma diminishes the humanity of that individual, generating fear, hostility, and anxiety. If, conversely, a dogma adds to one's spiritual, emotional, and intellectual life, then one may actually be enriched by studying the dogma.

For example, if the tradition sustains a belief in the centrality of prayer, as is true of all three traditions of the West, Judaism, Christianity, and Islam, that belief and practice not only transforms the individual but is also a basis for dialogue among the three faiths. The more genuine the prayer experience of the individuals in dialogue, the greater the possibility of interreligious respect and agreement among them.

A CAULDRON OF DIFFERENCES

The modern world has its own cauldron of differences. On one end of the spectrum is popular, secular culture. On the other end is religious fundamentalism, which will not concede the legitimacy of other people's beliefs concerning the Sacred. If a person is stuck in either end of the belief spectrum, she or he cannot move into the experiences of spirituality.

Spirituality changes perceptions. It is grounded in the middle of the spectrum. In the middle of the rainbow, we are able to believe enough so that we may take the plunge into mystery.

THE EXPERIENCE IN ITSELF MAY NOT CHANGE

Our external lives—for example, our jobs, friends, locations —may not change appreciably. What does change with increased wisdom, however, is how I approach my job, and how I treat and am treated by the people in my life. Life is gift, and the blessings of the Divine within and without illuminate my path as wisdom is born in my consciousness.

Medieval and Renaissance spirituality teaches the importance of living a life with a connection to the spiritual. "The purpose of learning is to grasp the divine," states the Jewish Kabbalah.[2]

That was the medieval view of learning. Learning was how one enriched his or her life by coming closer to the Divine. Actually, the Kabbalah's words are stronger: "to grasp the divine." Whether the upward-stretching spires of a Gothic cathedral, the energy pulsating in a Michelangelo sculpture, or the poignant parables of the medieval Islamic mystics, all shared that same goal, that same yearning: to grasp the Divine.

TINTORETTO'S MARY

On the outskirts of Venice lies Jacopo Tintoretto's (1518–1594) house and parish church, Madonna dell'Orto, one of the few places in Venice that still has the tweed cobblestones that once lined Saint Mark's Square. On entering the church, one sees Tintoretto's picture of Mary as a young girl: the *Presentation of Mary in the Temple* (fig. 10). There are many exquisite Madonna and Child paintings in Venice, especially Giovanni Bellini's, but they usually portray Mary as a very sorrowful, pensive, adult figure. This is justifiably so, because she is seeing the destiny of Jesus.

To view, instead, a painting of Mary as a young, vibrant girl-child, full of confidence and expectation, has a great deal to do with the magnetic appeal of the *Presentation of Mary in the Temple*. Tintoretto's Mary is full of joy. She is neither afraid nor reluctant to climb the temple's capacious steps for her presentation. She does this willingly, obviously trusting in God as she climbs the stairs with a gentle guiding hand from her mother, Saint Anne, into a new stage of development and transformation.

Mary is a symbol of the common meanings shared among the major Western religions. Mary is a young Jewish girl who comes to represent the beginning of Christianity. In the Middle Ages, she is revered as Notre Dame, Our Lady, and is prayed to as Mother of the Redeemed by Christians of the West. In Greek, for Christians of the Eastern rites and churches, Mary is *Theotokos*, the God-bearer: She who with open heart, spiritually welcomes the divine Word into matter bodily. Mary is also revered in Islamic tradition. In fact an entire chapter in the Qur'an is devoted to her (chapter 19; "Maryam"). Mary is Mother of the universe, but also each person's own spiritual mother. Mary is there to help us, guide us, steer us away from evil.

Tintoretto presents us with this young, innocent girl, full of hope and life. Mary has been with human beings culturally

Fig. 10: Tintoretto (1518–1594), *Presentation of Mary in the Temple* (detail).

for over two thousand years; some believe her spirit as Protectoress and Mother has been with us since the beginning of time. Mary is in the Presence. She demonstrates divine faith and obedience, and grows into becoming a free woman because she embodies peace and harmony by saying "Yes." Yes to God's will. Jews, Christians, and Muslims may attain peace and harmony only by going back metaphorically to this little child: one of their own.

Mary was a brave girl climbing those colossal steps. Tintoretto used to practice drawing his figures flying through time and space by modeling and creating wax models that he hung from the ceiling. He would study how sunlight, candlelight, and shadow played on the wax figures. Later, Tintoretto would recreate his studies of light and shadow in his immense paintings.

When he has Mary climbing the steps, they look enormous to us as we look up at her from the floor in the church. She seems so small, but full of strength and poise, the epitome of curiosity and inner trust, a David in this Goliath of an experience.

UNCONDITIONAL LOVE

Mary knew God was with her, even when she faced a monumental experience. She was still so connected to divine consciousness that when she grew up and became a mother she would not even have to think about what that look meant as she gazed into her son's eyes.

Mary understood that look of unconditional love. She would always be there for Jesus: Jesus born into a Jewish heritage, Son of God for Christians, and esteemed prophet for Muslims (Qur'an 3:3).

That look in countless paintings of Madonna and Child was prophetic of Jesus' entire life and teaching: "This is my commandment, that you love one another as I have loved you" (John 15:12).

NOTES

CHAPTER 1

1. Michelangelo, *Last Judgment*, fresco on the altar wall of the Sistine Chapel, 1534–1541.

2. Georges Duby, *The Age of the Cathedrals: 980–1420*, trans. E. Levieux and B. Thompson (Chicago: University of Chicago Press, 1981), 100.

3. Ibid., 105.

4. Grünewald's real name, according to modern scholars, was either Mathis Gothardt or Gothardt Neithardt. However, since the "incorrect" name Mathias Grünewald has been used for five hundred years, the artist is still known as Mathias Grünewald.

5. Stanley Meisler, "A Masterpiece Born of Saint Anthony's Fire," *Smithsonian*, October 1999, 80.

6. Ibid., 71.

7. Helen Gardner, Richard G. Tansey and Fred S. Kleiner, *Gardner's Art through the Ages*, 10th ed. (Fort Worth: Harcourt Brace College Publishers, 1996), 793.

8. Modern scholarship believes that the nails were most probably placed in the wrists in order to keep the body from pulling off the cross from its own weight, which would surely have occurred if the nails had been hammered into the centers of the palms.

9. Dante, *Il Purgatorio*, trans. John Ciardi (London: Penguin Books, 1961), XI: 94–96.

10. Rachel Jacoff, ed., *The Cambridge Companion to Dante* (Cambridge: Cambridge University Press, 1993), 8.

11. Ibid., 11.

12. Dante Alighieri, *The Inferno*, trans. John Ciardi (London: Penguin Books, 1982), xiv. From the historical introduction by Archibald MacAllister.

13. Bonaventure, *Minor Life of St. Francis* Chapter 3: Sixth Lesson, in Marion A. Habig, ed., *St. Francis of Assisi: Writings and Early Biographies; English Omnibus of the Sources for the Life of St. Francis* (Chicago: Franciscan Herald Press, 1983), 808–809.

14. Bonaventure, *Major Life of St. Francis*, VIII: 9, in *The Message of St. Francis, with Frescoes from the Basilica of St. Francis of Assisi*, ed. Sister Nan, (New York: Penguin Studio, 1998), 30.

15. Ibid.

16. Bernard McGinn, *The Growth of Mysticism: Gregory the Great through the 12th Century* (New York: Crossroad, 1996), 357.

17. Ibid.

18. Guigo II, *The Ladder of Monks, A Letter on the Contemplative Life and Twelve Meditations*, trans. Edmund College and James Walsh (Kalamazoo, MI: Cistercian Publications, 1981), 67–68.

19. Ibid.

20. Ibid.

21. McGinn, *Growth of Mysticism*, 358.

22. Guigo II, *Ladder of Monks*, 68.

23. Harvey Egan, SJ, *An Anthology of Christian Mysticism* (Collegeville, MN: Liturgical Press, 1991), 386.

24. Julian of Norwich, *Showings*, Classics of Western Spirituality, trans. Edmund College and James Walsh (New York: Paulist Press, 1977), 151.

25. Egan, *Anthology of Christian Mysticism*, 386.

26. Grace Jantzen, *Julian of Norwich: Mystic and Theologian* (New York: Paulist Press, 1988), 35.

27. Ibid.

28. Ibid.

29. Ibid., 145–146.

30. Julian of Norwich, *Revelations of Divine Love*, trans. Clifton Wolters (New York: Penguin, 1984), 35.

31. Bernard McGinn, "The English Mystics," in *Christian Spirituality: High Middle Ages and Reformation*, eds. Jill Raitt, John Meyendorff, and Bernard McGinn. vol. 17, *World Spirituality: An Encyclopedic History of the Religious Quest*. (New York: Crossroad, 1987), 204.

32. Julian of Norwich, *Revelations*, 170.

33. Julian of Norwich, *Showings*, 183.

34. Julian of Norwich, *Showings*, 342–43.

35. Ibid.

36. Ibid.

37. Ibid.

38. Ibid.

39. Julian of Norwich, *Revelations*, 167.

40. Ibid.

CHAPTER 2

1. Teresa of Avila, Letter, 22 October 1577, quoted in *The Interior Castle*, trans. Kieran Kavanaugh and Otilio Rodriguez, The Classics of Western Spirituality (New York, Paulist Press, 1979), 18.

2. *Biblioteca Mistica Carmelitana*, ed. Silverio de Santa Teresa, Vol. 18 (Burgos: Tipografia de "El Monte Carmelo," 1934), 315.

3. Teresa of Avila, *The Interior Castle*, vol. 2 of *The Collected Works of Saint Teresa of Avila*, trans. Kieran Kavanaugh and Otilio Rodriguez (Washington, DC: Institute of Carmelite Studies, 1980), 447.

4. Ibid., 266.

5. Ibid., 430.

6. Ibid., 413.

7. Ibid., 412.

8. Ibid., 401.

9. Ibid.

10. Ibid., 400.

11. Ibid., 284.

12. Ibid.

13. Ibid., 286.

14. Teresa of Avila, *The Interior Castle*, trans. Kavanaugh and Rodriguez, The Classics of Western Spirituality (New York: Paulist Press, 1979) 1:6, see n. 7.

15. "For even though they are very involved in the world, they have good desires and sometimes, though only once in a while, they entrust themselves to our Lord and reflect on who they are, although in a rather hurried fashion. During the period of a month they will sometimes pray, but their minds are then filled with business matters that ordinarily occupy them. They are so attached to these things that where their treasure lies their heart goes also." Ibid., 39.

16. Ibid., 41.

17. Ibid., 53.

18. Ibid.

19. Ibid., 58.

20. Ibid., 65.

21. Ibid., 78.

22. Ibid.

23. Ibid., 78.

24. This is one of the founding concepts in Buddhism. See Wm. Theodore de Bary, *The Buddhist Tradition in India, China, and Japan* (New York: Random House, 1972), 9: "Basic is the doctrine of the 'Four Noble Truths': 1) that all life is inevitably sorrowful; 2) that sorrow is due to craving; 3) that it can only be stopped by the stopping of craving; and 4) and this can only be

done by a course of carefully disciplined and moral conduct, culminating in the life of concentration and meditation."

25. Teresa of Avila, *Interior Castle*, trans. Kavanaugh and Rodriguez, 71.

26. Ibid., 79.

27. Ibid., 343.

28. Ibid., 420.

29. Ibid., 426.

30. Ibid., 426.

31. Ibid.

32. Ibid., 435.

33. Ibid., 435.

34. Ibid., 433.

35. Ibid., 442.

36. See Robert E. Fisher, *Buddhist Art and Architecture* (London: Thames & Hudson, 1993) for examples.

37. Teresa of Avila, *Interior Castle*, trans. Kavanaugh and Rodriguez, 450.

CHAPTER 3

1. Daniel C. Matt, "The Mystic and the Mizwot," in *Jewish Spirituality I: From the Bible through the Middle Ages*, vol. 13, *World Spirituality: An Encyclopedic History of the Religious Quest*, ed. Arthur Green (New York: Crossroad, 1996), 386.

2. There is recent scholarship on the relationship between Rabbi Simeon bar Yohai's spiritual ideas and Moses de León's writing of the Zohar. One valuable text on Jewish mysticism is *The Schocken Book of Jewish Mystical Testimonies* compiled with commentary by Louis Jacobs (New York: Schocken Books, 1996). See the chapter, "The Zohar on the High Priest's Ecstasy," 100–108.

See also Gershom Scholem, *Major Trends in Jewish Mysticism*, 3rd rev. ed. (New York: Schocken Books, 1961),

156–204; Zohar, *The Book of Enlightenment*, trans. Daniel C. Matt, The Classics of Western Spirituality (Mahwah, NJ: Paulist Press, 1983), 3–10, 25–32; Yehuda Liebes, "How the Zohar Was Written," in *Studies in the Zohar* (Albany: State University of New York, 1993) 85–138.

3. Liebes, 101.

4. Note that the theology of God's transcendence is more pronounced in Judaism and Islam than in Christianity. Christianity, because of Jesus' incarnation, has a Christology that equally emphasizes God as transcendent and God as immanent in creation.

5. According to my esteemed colleague, Professor Emeritus Robert Platzner, *safar* in Hebrew means, "to count, to unite, to tell, to cut."

6. Lawrence Fine, trans., *Safed Spirituality: Rules of Mystical Piety. The Beginning of Wisdom*, The Classics of Western Spirituality (New York: Paulist Press, 1984), 159.

7. *The Early Kabbalah*, trans. Ronald C. Kiener, ed. and introd. Joseph Dan, The Classics of Western Spirituality (New York/Mahwah: Paulist Press, 1986), 8.

8. Ibid., 13.

9. Ibid., 8.

10. *Safed Spirituality*, 159.

11. Daniel C. Matt, *The Essential Kabbalah: The Heart of Jewish Mysticism* (San Francisco: HarperSanFrancisco, 1996), 67.

12. Ibid., 32.

13. *Safed Spirituality*, 159.

14. Matt, *The Essential Kabbalah*, 125.

15. Ibid., 132.

16. *Safed Spirituality*, 159. By contrast, the Taoist Yang is male intelligence and activity; Yin is feminine intuition and receptivity.

17. Ibid.

18. Ibid., 160.

19. Gershom G. Scholem, *On the Kabbalah and Its Symbolism* (New York: Schocken, 1965), 150.

20. Genesis 1:26.

21. Matt, *The Essential Kabbalah*, 17.

22. This example and others in the book come from students in class during twenty-five years of college teaching. I think they are important examples to mention in order to bring what might be abstract spiritual ideas into the realm of popular American culture.

23. Matt, *The Essential Kabbalah*, 31.

24. Ibid., 24.

CHAPTER 4

1. Emile Mâle, *The Gothic Image: Religious Art in France of the Thirteenth Century*, trans. Dora Nussey (New York: Harper, 1958), 82.

2. Ibid.

3. Ibid., 84. See also Marilyn Stokstad, *Medieval Art* (Oxford: Westview Press, 1988); Christopher Wilson, *The Gothic Cathedral: The Architecture of the Great Church, 1130–1530* (London: Thames & Hudson, 1990); Paul Frankl and Paul Crossley, *Gothic Architecture* (New Haven: Yale University Press, 2000); Paul Williamson, *Gothic Sculpture, 1140–1300* (New Haven: Yale University Press, 1995). See also "Les Cathédrales: Un lieu de vie au Moyen Age," a lovely volume of *Historia Thématique*, n. 74, November–December 2001.

4. Ibid., 88.

5. Ibid.

6. Malcolm B. Miller, Sonia Halliday, and Laura Lushington, *Chartres Cathedral* (Andover, UK: Pitkin Guides, 1996), 18. See also Sir Banister Fletcher, *A History of Architecture*, 20th ed. (London: Architectural Press, 1996).

7. *Suger on the Abbey Church of St.-Denis and Its Art Treasures* (Princeton: Princeton University Press, 1946), 95.

8. George Duby, *The Age of the Cathedrals: Art and Society 980–1420*, trans. E. Levieux and B. Thompson (Chicago: University of Chicago Press, 1983), 99.

9. Suger, *De Administratione*, in *Abbot Suger on the Abbey Church of St.-Denis and Its Art Treasures*, trans. Erwin Panofsky and Gerda Panofsky-Soergel (Princeton: Princeton University Press, 1979), 63–64. The Biblical quotation is Ezekiel 27:13.

10. For example, at Laon cathedral sixteen oxen are carved in the highest tower. See Williamson's *Gothic Sculpture*.

CHAPTER 5

1. The quote in the chapter title is from Dante Alighieri, *The Inferno*, translated by John Ciardi (New York: Penguin, 1982), XXXIV: 143.

2. We do have Boccaccio's description of Dante, which aside from the dark curly hair and beard, seems to match Giotto's portrait: a long face, aquiline nose, with a melancholy, reflective character.

3. Ciardi, *The Inferno*, XV.

4. Dante Alighieri, *The Divine Comedy of Dante Alighieri*, trans. Henry Cary (Cambridge: Harvard Classics, 1980), XXXIII: 138.

5. W. S. Merwin in the Foreword to his translation of the *Purgatorio* comments on the history of the troubadours in Italy: "The rhymed and highly stylized poetry of the troubadour, with its allegiance to music, the codes of the courts of love, the Hispano-Arabic assimilation of the philosophy of classical Greece, were essentials of the great Provencal civilization of the twelfth and early thirteenth centuries…that rich, generous, brilliant tradition…were part of Dante's heritage….The legacy of the

troubadours survived even beyond Dante. Petrarch is sometimes described as the last of the troubadours," xvi.

6. Dante Alighieri, *Purgatorio*, translated by W. S. Merwin (New York: Alfred A. Knopf, 2000), XXXIII: 142–144.

7. Jorge Luis Borga, "The Divine Comedy," in *Seven Nights*, trans. Eliot Weinberger (New York: New Directions, 1984), 13.

8. Bice was a common nickname for girls, including Dante's daughter, Antonia.

9. Dante Alighieri, *Paradiso*, trans. John Ciardi (New York: Penguin, 1970), XX: 73–78.

10. Dante Alighieri, *Paradiso*, trans. John Sinclair (New York: Oxford University Press, 1961). XX: 73–78.

11. *Paradiso*, trans. Ciardi, XXVII: 103–105.

12. *Paradiso*, trans. Ciardi, XXXIII: 126.

13. *Paradiso*, trans. Sinclair, XXXIII: 140.

14. Avicenna (980–1037) and Averroes (1126–1198). Dante was familiar with both of these thinkers whose commentaries on Aristotle were extremely influential in the Latin West. See David E. Luscombe, *Medieval Thought*. Vol. 2, *A History of Western Philosophy* (Oxford: Oxford University Press, 1997).

15. Dante, trans. Cary, *The Divine Comedy*, IV: 112–114: "There dwelt a race, who slow their eyes around / Majestically moved, and in their port / Bore eminent authority: they spake / Seldom, but all their words were tuneful sweet."

16. Dante, *The Inferno*, trans. Ciardi, Canto III: 9. Michael Palma's translation, *Inferno* (New York: W. W. Norton & Company, 2002) reads "All you who enter, let no hope survive."

17. *The Divine Comedy*, trans. Cary: "This miserable fate / Suffer the wretched souls of those, who lived / Without or praise or blame," III: 32, 33.

18. Ibid., XXXIV: 136–143.

CHAPTER 6

1. Hildegard of Bingen, "Antiphon for the Trinity" in *Symphonia: A Critical Edition of the Symphony of the Harmony of Celestial Revelations*, trans. Barbara Newman (Ithaca: Cornell University Press, 1988), 143.

2. For example, see Sequentia's BMG/DHM recordings of the complete works of Hildegard of Bingen.

3. She was also a playwright. See for example, Bruce W. Hozeski, "Hildegard of Bingen's *Ordo Virtutum*: The Earliest Discovered Liturgical Morality Play," *American Benedictine Review* 26:3 (1975): 251–259.

4. She credited Volmar, and her later secretaries, with correcting her textual Latin.

5. Godefridus, monk, *The Life of Holy Hildegard by the Monks Gottfried and Theoderic*, ed. Mary Palmquist, Adelgundis Führkkötter, and John Kulas (Collegeville, MN: Liturgical Press, 1995), 3.

6. For an interesting study, see Eileen Power, *Medieval Women* (Cambridge: Cambridge University Press, 1997), especially chaps. 4 and 5. See also Katharina A. Wilson, editor, *Women Medieval Writers* (Athens: University of Georgia Press, 1984).

7. Renate Craine, *Hildegard: Prophet of the Cosmic Christ* (New York: Crossroad, 1997), 26–27.

8. Abbot Bernard of Clairvaux to Hildegard (1147) in *The Life*, ed. Palmquist, 103.

9. Craine, *Hildegard*, 26.

10. Hildegard of Bingen, *Scivias, Vita S. Hildegardis*, edited by J.-P. Migne, *Patrologia Latina* (Paris, 1855).

11. Hildegard of Bingen, *Scivias*, trans. Mother Columba Hart and Jane Bishop, Classics of Western Spirituality (New York: Paulist Press, 1990). From the Preface by Caroline Walker Bynum, 5. See also Caroline Walker Bynum, " '...And Woman His Humanity': Female Imagery in the Religious Writing of the

Later Middle Ages," in *Gender and Religion: On the Complexity of Symbols*, edited by C. W. Bynum, S. Harrell and P. Richman (Boston: Beacon Press, 1986), 257–88.

12. Ibid., 9. See also, for example, Kent Kraft, "The German Visionary: Hildegard of Bingen," in Wilson, *Medieval Women Writers*, 112. Hildegard undertook "what was for a woman of her time, indeed of any time, a singular and extraordinary venture, the first of a series of preaching tours that would lead her as far away as Bamberg and Zwiefalten."

13. Barbara Newman, *Sister of Wisdom: St. Hildegard's Theology of the Feminine* (Berkeley: University of California Press, 1987), 17–18.

14. Kraft, "German Visionary," 107.

15. Hildegard of Bingen, *Scivias*, trans. Mother Columba Hart and Jane Bishop. *Declaration*, 60. See also Elizabeth Petroff, ed., *Medieval Women's Visionary Literature* (Oxford: Oxford University Press, 1986), 32–44. And, Barbara J. Newman, "Divine Power Made Perfect in Weakness: St. Hildegard on the Frail Sex," in *Peaceweavers*, vol. 2 *Medieval Religious Women*, ed. Lillian T. Shank and John Nichols (Kalamazoo, MI: Cistercian Publications: 1987), 103–22.

16. In Christian tradition, statues and paintings representing the Sacred Heart of Jesus have one palm raised in the "Fear not" gesture; the other hand touches Jesus' heart. The essence of the Christian message is "Fear not, it is I," for God is love as expressed by the Sacred Heart.

17. "Hildegard's visions are in fact one vision: a primer and a *summa* of Christian doctrine." Bynum, Preface, *Scivias*, 5.

18. Edward P. Nolan, *Cry Out and Write: A Feminine Poetics of Revelation* (New York: Continuum, 1994), 20.

19. Photosynthesis = "in botany, the formation of carbohydrates in living plants from water and carbon dioxide, by the

action of sunlight on the chlorophyll." Webster's Deluxe Unabridged Dictionary, 2nd Edition.

20. Hildegard von Bingen, *Canticles of Ecstasy*, Cologne Sequentia Ensemble for Medieval Music, compact disc, Deutsche Harmonia Mundi, 1994.

21. Hildegard, *Scivias*, trans. Hart and Bishop, 124.

22. Hildegard of Bingen, *Holistic Healing*, trans. Mary Palmquist, John Kulas, and Patrick Madigan, SJ (Collegeville, MN: Liturgical Press, 1994), xiii.

23. *Holistic Healing* offers examples of both preventative health measures written and administered by Hildegard and what to take prescriptively for specific illnesses, which Hildegard elaborates on in some detail.

24. Ibid., xii.

25. Craine, *Hildegard*. From *Welt und Mensch (De operatione Dei)* IV, 19. Craine's translation, 84.

26. Ibid., IX, 2. Craine's translation, 133.

27. Ibid., *Heilkunde*, 83.

28. Bede Griffiths, *The Marriage of East and West* (London: William Collins, 1982), 35.

29. Craine, *Hildegard*. From *Scivias*, III, p. 140. For more on the theme of the "Heavenly Jerusalem," see the chapter, "Building Wisdom's House in History."

30. Ibid. See also Miriam Schmitt, "Hildegard of Bingen: Leaves of God's Justice," in *Cistercian Studies*, vol. XXIV, (1989:1): 69–88.

31. *Sophia* = wisdom in Greek.

32. Newman, *Symphonia*, p. 151.

33. Ibid.

34. Hildegard, *Holistic Healing*, xv.

CHAPTER 7

1. "Rabi'a al-Adawiyya's Devotion to God," was originally published in *Journal of Dharma*, Volume XV, No. 3, Devotions in World Religions, July–September 1990: 232–239. There is a vast selection of texts on Islam and the mystics of Islam, the Sufis, available now in English. Some helpful examples are: John L. Esposito, *Islam: The Straight Path*, updated with new epilogue, 3rd ed. (New York: Oxford University Press, 2004); Seyyed Hossein Nasr, editor, *Islamic Spirituality*, Volume 19 & 20 in *World Spirituality: An Encyclopedic History of the Religious Quest* (New York: Crossroad, 1997); *Early Islamic Mysticism: Sufi, Qur'an, Miraj, Poetic and Theological Writings*, trans. and ed. Michael A. Sells, Classics of Western Spirituality (New York/Mahwah: Paulist Press, 1995; and *Knowledge of God in Classic Sufism*, trans. and introd. John Renard, Classics of Western Spirituality (New York/Mahwah, Paulist Press, 2004). For more on Rabi'a and Islamic Spirituality, see Maria Jaoudi, *Christian and Islamic Spirituality: Sharing a Journey* (Mahwah, NJ: Paulist Press, 1993).

2. Rabi'a al-Adawiyya, *Doorkeeper of the Heart: Versions of Rabi'a*, trans. Charles Upton (Vermont: Threshold, 1987), 10–11. Muslim legend has it that Ibrahim Ibn Adham was a prince who gave up his throne and became a wandering dervish. It is not fair to point to Ibrahim as opposed to devotional love, since his path incorporated the prayer of focusing on God's merciful name and was simply different from Rabi'a's in orientation.

3. Idries Shah, *The Sufis*, with an Introduction by Robert Graves (Garden City, NY: Doubleday, 1971), quoting Rabi'a, 185.

4. See, Margaret Smith, *Rabi'a the Mystic and Her Fellow Saints in Islam* (Cambridge: Cambridge University Press, 1928).

5. Annemarie Schimmel, *Mystical Dimensions of Islam* (Chapel Hill: University of North Carolina Press, 1978), 40.

6. Upton, 30.

7. Ibid., 30.

8. Schimmel, 39.

9. Widad El Sakkakini, *First Among the Sufis: The Life and Thought of Rabi'a al-Adawiyya*, translated by Nabil Safwat, with an Introduction by Doris Lessing (London: Octagon Press, 1982), 70.

10. Upton, 41.

11. Cf. Philip Hitti, *History of the Arabs*, 9th ed. (New York: St. Martin's Press, 1967), 77.

12. Nancy Goldberger and Jill Tarule, *Women's Ways of Knowing* (New York: Basic Books, 1986), 217–19.

13. Upton, 11.

14. Ibid., 48.

15. Cf. *Qur'an* 51:20–21: "And in the earth are signs to those of real faith, and in yourselves. What! Do you not see?" *Al-Qur'an*, trans. Ahmad Ali (Princeton: Princeton University Press, 1988).

16. Schimmel, 358.

17. Philip Dunn, Manuela Dunn-Mascetti, and R. A. Nicholson, *The Illustrated Rumi: A Treasury of Wisdom from the Poet of the Soul*. Foreword by Huston Smith (San Francisco: HarperSanFrancisco, 2000), 7. From Huston Smith's Foreword: "…we have Jalalu'ddin Rumi, who eight centuries after his death, has been for almost a decade the best-selling poet in America."

18. William C. Chittick, *The Sufi Path of Love: The Spiritual Teachings of Rumi*. SUNY Series in Islamic Spirituality edited by Seyyed Hossein Nasr (Albany: State University of New York Press, 1983), 2.

19. *Mystical Poems of Rumi*, trans. A. J. Arberry (Chicago: University of Chicago Press, 1968), poem 47, p. 42.

20. Ibid., 3.

21. "When Shamsi met Rumi he took his books and threw them in a pool of water saying 'Now you must live what you know.' " *Rumi: Divani Shamsi Tabriz*, ed. and trans. Reynold A Nicholson (San Francisco: Rainbow Bridge (originally published by Cambridge University Press), 1973), 12.

22. Sunni Muslims comprise 80 percent of the global population of Islam. Sunnis believe that Muhammad's successors are to be elected by the Muslim community. Shi'ite Muslims are in the minority and believe that Muhammad's successors derive from the immediate descendents of Muhammad's own family. This lineage begins with his cousin and son-in-law, 'Ali. 'Ali was married to Fatima, Muhammad's favorite daughter. Shi'ites are extremely devoted to these familial descendents including the two sons of Fatima and 'Ali, Hasan and Husayn.

23. Arberry, *Mystical Poems*, poem 31, p. 32.

24. Ibid., poem 50, p. 45.

25. Chittick, 2.

26. Nicholson, *Rumi: Divani Shamsi Tabriz*, poem XXIII, p. 62.

27. Arberry, *Mystical Poems*, poem 47, p. 42.

28. Idries Shah, *The Sufis*, introduction by Robert Graves (New York: Doubleday, 1971), 357.

29. Jaoudi, 33.

30. Arberry, *Mystical Poems*, poem 49, p. 43.

31. Chittick, translations from *Diwan-i Shams-i Tabrizi*, poem 21565, p. 290.

32. Ibid., poems 32022–23, p. 290.

33. R. Foltz, F. Denny, A. Baharuddin, editors, *Islam and Ecology: A Bestowed Trust* (Cambridge, MA: Center for the Study of World Religions, Harvard Divinity School, 2003), see chapter by L. Clarke, "The Universe Alive: Nature in the Masnavi of Jalal al-Din Rumi," 60.

34. Seyyed Hossein Nasr, *Islamic Art and Spirituality* (Albany: State University of New York Press, 1987), 142.

35. Arberry, *Mystical Poems*, poem 106, p. 91.

36. Huston Smith, foreword to *The Illustrated Rumi*, trans. Philip Dunn, M. D. Mascetti, and R. A. Nicholson (San Francisco: HarperOne, 2000), 7.

37. Ibid., 94.

CHAPTER 8

1. *Sfumato* is a term Leonardo da Vinci coined to describe a painting technique that blends tones and colors so softly that it produces a hazy, mysterious quality.

2. In Leonardo's drawing, "God's Intellect," on the function of neck muscles to support the neck, Leonardo writes: "rejoice that our God has devoted his intellect to the perfection of this tool." Leonardo da Vinci's Notebooks, 19075v, Royal Library at Windsor.

3. Michelangelo, *The Complete Poems of Michelangelo*, trans. John Nims (Chicago: University of Chicago Press, 1998) poem 250, p. 195–196.

4. See Franco Cesati, *The Medici: Story of a European Dynasty* (Florence: La Madragora, 1999), 45.

5. Michelangelo, *Complete Poems*, 180. The poem was actually a reply to the quotation by Giovanni di Carlo Strozzi on *Night*:

> The Night you see in graceful sleep, we know
> was carved in marble by an angel here.
> In sleep—that means she's living. You appear
> doubtful? Then wake her up. She'll talk to you.

6. Ibid., #247, 124.

7. Sir Banister Fletcher, *A History of Architecture*, 20th ed. (London: Architectural Press, 1998), 247.

8. Giorgio Vasari, *Lives of the Artists: A Selection*, trans. George Bull (Baltimore: Penguin, 1987), Volume I, 137.

9. Ibid.

10. Ibid., 133.

11. Ibid., 133–134.

12. Ibid., 138.

13. Ibid., 139.

14. Deuteronomy 32:12.

15. Matthew 6:10.

16. Ibid., 27.

17. Among Giovanni della Robbia's most well-known works is the lavabo of the sacristy (1497–99) in the entrance to the Sacristy of Santa Maria Novella. See Aldo Tarquini, OP, *Santa Maria Novella* (Florence: Becocci, 2000), 54–56.

18. Available at http://www.all-art.org/early_renaissance/botticelli15.html.

19. Paul O. Kristeller, trans. Virginia Conant, *The Philosophy of Marsilio Ficino* (New York: Columbia University Press, 1943), 95. See, also Dominic O'Meara, ed., *Neoplatonism and Christian Thought* (Norfolk, VA: International Society for Neoplatonic Studies, 1982). Distributed by State University of New York Press.

CHAPTER 9

1. Popular culture is an area of academic research and the topic of numerous books, including: Lawrence Grossberg, Ellen Wartella, D. Whitney, *Media Making: Mass Media in a Popular Culture* (Thousand Oaks, CA: Sage Publications, 1998); John Storey, *Cultural Studies and the Study of Popular Culture* (Athens: University of Georgia, 2003); John Storey, *Inventing Popular Culture* (Oxford: Blackwell, 2003); Dominic Strinati, *An Introduction to Studying Popular Culture* (London: Routledge, 2000); Jon Pahl, *Shopping Malls and Other Sacred Places* (Grand Rapids, MI:

Brazos Press, 2003); Sharon Zukin, *Point of Purchase: How Shopping Changed American Culture* (New York: Routledge, 2005); Toby Miller, *Cultural Citizenship: Cosmopolitanism, Consumerism, and Television in a Neoliberal Age* (Philadelphia: Temple University Press, 2006).

2. Daniel C. Matt, *Zohar: The Book of Enlightenment*, Classics of Western Spirituality (Mahwah, NJ: Paulist Press, 1983), 21.

INDEX